A Toast to Martinborough and the Wairarapa

CW01424863

a Toast

to Martinborough and the Wairarapa

Stories from the Vineyards

Dave Cull

Longacre Press

Longacre Press and Dave Cull gratefully acknowledge the generous support and sponsorship of Toast Martinborough.

TOAST
MARTINBOROUGH

This book is copyright. Apart from any fair dealing for the purpose of private study, research, criticism or review, as permitted under the Copyright Act, no part may be reproduced by any process without prior permission of Longacre Press and the author.

Dave Cull asserts his moral right to be identified as the author of this work.

© Dave Cull

ISBN 1 877135 78 X

First published by Longacre Press, 2003
9 Dowling Street, Dunedin, New Zealand

Book cover and design by Christine Buess
Printed by Rainbow Print, Christchurch

page 2: Palliser Estate. *Pam Ryan*

Contents

For Willie Brown and Bill Brink. Pinot-impassioned to the end.

Acknowledgements

My biggest thankyou must go to all those people whose words make up so much, and by far the most interesting parts, of this book. Thank you for your time, your hospitality in many cases, and your insights and stories. I thoroughly enjoyed our conversations.

Thanks to Lawrie Bryant for his initial suggestion that I write the book, for those first introductions, and for his and Sally's warm hospitality at Wycroft. Thanks also to John and Philippa Falloon who very generously had me to stay at Bowlands House, and who opened yet other doors as well.

The bulk of my research naturally centred around Martinborough. While I was there, Clive and Phyll at Ata Rangi took me into their whanau. I could not have achieved the amount I did without their generous, inclusive hospitality and friendship. Thanks too to Olly and Alison for the bounty of their table and convivial company.

Gareth Winter at the Wairarapa Archive in Masterton combines an encyclopedic mind, bursting enthusiasm for his historical enquiries, and an utterly open-handed attitude to anyone who asks for information. Gareth was most helpful, as were the staff at the Masterton Library who guided me to material I was unaware of. Thank you all.

I'm also very grateful to Rosemary Chifney who loaned me news cuttings that provided all sorts of clues and confirmations.

I helped out at a couple of wineries, and gained a little of their working flavour. So a big thanks to Strat Canning, Clive Paton and Grant Stanley for tolerating my 'assistance'.

I very much appreciate everything Toast Martinborough did in supporting my endeavour; and in the midst of the myriad things she doubtless had to attend to in the lead up to Toast 2002, Cath Hopkin found time to facilitate our attendance. Cheers.

Finally, my appreciation to the people with whom I have collaborated in putting this book together. The photographers have done a wonderful job; I especially wish to thank Pam Ryan for her portrayal of not only the district but the people. Thanks to Emma Neale for her considered, thorough and perceptive editing, to Christine Buess for a great design job, and to Barbara Larson and Annette Riley for their support, guidance and damn good company. The Longacre team were, again, utterly professional and a joy to work with.

Road over the Rimutakas. *David Wall*

Prologue

The trickle of cars starts around 4 p.m. on Friday, before the Capital's working week is even officially over: Wellingtonians with holiday homes on the plain are heading away before the rush. The flow builds as dusk falls; an intermittent line of headlights twisting and turning up the serpentine high road to the hinterland.

Provincial MPs, heading home from the Beehive's drone, wade through airport departure lounges against an atypical stream of weekend visitors arriving from Dunedin, Marlborough, Auckland, Queenstown: anywhere too far to drive.

People pour onto the plain from the north too. Even more come on Saturday: from Hawkes Bay, Gisborne, and farther afield; including overseas contingents. By Saturday evening there's not a spare bed to be had within a forty kilometre radius.

But Sunday morning brings the real thing. Trains and scores of buses disgorge thousands of festive visitors. They're keen too. Tickets sold out within an hour some months ago, and ten and a half thousand punters paid $50 each to be here. On average they'll spend twice that again on food and drink over the course – or should that be courses – of the day.

It's the third Sunday in November, for more than a decade the day of Toast Martinborough: the biggest, boldest, most celebrated wine and food festival in the country. How did this happen? How did a tiny town in the provincial backwater that was – the Wairarapa – get to achieve this level of magnetism?

The Wairarapa is Wellington's back garden, just over the city's fractured garden wall, the Rimutaka Range. It's an ancient garden, fruitful for both early Maori, and for European settlers. Kupe, the legendary Polynesian progenitor of Aoteoroa, reputedly named the area, and his canoes are immortalised in a line of hills, Nga Waka-o-Kupe (The Canoes of Kupe) east of Greytown.

Others claim the wandering tohunga Hau named Lake Wairarapa (glistening water) in the nineteenth century. Whoever was responsible, early Europeans were so tongue-tied by its pronunciation, they substituted Wyderop.

The bulk of the region is broken hill country, but a long broad valley, formed over eons by the Ruamahanga River and its numerous tributaries runs north-east from the roaring surf of Palliser Bay in the south. These rivers filled in a previously submerged inlet, helped perhaps by the vigorous tectonic faults that rive the region and from some five million years ago, threw up the mountainous spine that cuts off the Wairarapa from the Tasman Sea.

In pre-European times, Lake Wairarapa abounded in eels: the surrounding swampland in wild fowl. The area was a larder for the tangata whenua, Ngati Kahu-ngunu. Indirectly those eels attracted European settlers. During a prolonged and severe drought around 1600, a fire set by Maori fishermen to dry eels spread and swept through much of the low-lying valley. Nearly quarter of a millennium later, when Europeans arrived, the area was still largely bereft of bush, and perfect for sheep grazing. One of the earliest run-holders, Daniel Riddiford, signed his first lease with local Maori in 1846. As the countryside was taken up by sheep-men, towns like Greytown, Carterton, Featherston and Masterton were established by the Small Farms Association, or the provincial government, as the road from Wellington pushed north.

Cleared for four centuries, and farmed for nearly half that, the Wairarapa plain now has a comfortable, lived-on demeanour. Tall northern hemisphere oaks and firs sway quietly in old churchyards. Farms are ordered and neat, like the roads. Arrow-straight shelter belts and trim hedges hem swards of pasture.

East from the main north road, towards the hills, the land becomes a little more rumpled. Roads meander around hillocks and through cuttings, then drop off river terraces only to climb out again once the inevitable bridge has been crossed. Lone totara stand in paddocks musing on past company, the split bones of their kindred surrounding them: yoked in regular lines by strands of fencing wire.

Although it's the driest region of the North Island, parts of the area have the unmistakable look of 'soggy bottom': patches of swamp only partially drained. Thick mud cloys roads where dairy herds cross on their way to milking. Yet other parts are parched, gravelly river terrace that in summer wouldn't support a dry wether.

Martinborough, on the eastern edge of the broad Ruamahanga flood plain, is set in a wide saucer rimmed with low hills. Pine and poplar shelter belts criss-cross the flats, while the denuded hills have the shaved, pleated appearance that clearing for grazing leaves. Willows line the streams: toi-tois the ditches. It's pastoral country, and long tubes of green plastic bailage lie fat and ripe along fences, like gigantic pupae. Apart from an odd square of lighter, limier green around the town, nothing suggests you'd find anything more here than fat lamb, dairy and beef cattle.

Farmland near Martinborough.

David Wall

Chardonnay:

luscious, biscuity and bursting with peach and hazelnut characters.

Riesling:

succulent, limey, aging gracefully for a decade.

Sauvignon Blanc:

minerally and bone-dry; or hinting sweetly
of passionfruit and melon.

Gewürztraminer:

a perfumed medley of ginger, spice and stone fruit.

Botrytised dessert wine:

intense, engorged with honeyed amber.

Pinot Gris:

a ripe concentration of lychees and pears.

Cabernet red:

mysterious, swirling with plum, spice, mint and cassis.

Pinot Noir:

truly glorious, the prince among reds: darkly opulent, complex and
stuffed with savoury, fragrant fruit and mushroomy lasciviousness.

That's what you'll find here. This drought-prone backwater, a tortuous drive over that notorious road from Wellington, has emerged from obscurity to become the fine wine mecca of New Zealand. The Wairarapa has only 3.6 per cent of the nation's grapes, yet it consistently wins a hugely disproportionate share of medals and accolades across more varieties than any other region.

From the 20/20 viewpoint of the present, Wairarapa's glittering vinous ascendancy, might not seem surprising. The region should be in with a chance, you'd say. It is, after all, a pearl in the string of wine regions along the snug eastern rain shadow of New Zealand's mountainous backbone. Fly in a straight line north-east from Central Otago to Gisborne, and you'll pass over more than 90 per cent of New Zealand's vineyards. The Wairarapa is pretty much in the middle, and being the driest area in the North Island, it's perfect wine territory. We know that now.

But thirty years ago it was quite a different spectacle. Flying up from the south then, you'd have been a tedious halfway through your journey before spotting the first vines: the tentative greening of Montana's pioneering grapes in Marlborough. The straight vine lines in an otherwise irregular landscape might have given them away. But you'd have been above Hawkes Bay before you caught even a whiff of fermentation on the wind. Wine-wise, Wairarapa was a blank.

New Zealand's early wine development took no cognisance of the suitability of place. The imperatives for grape planting were largely cultural. If people hailed from wine-making cultures, they planted grapes wherever they happened to settle. Mostly that happened to be around Auckland and in Northland. There were however exceptions to that cultural connection rule: the Wairarapa among them.

Lansdowne Vineyard – William Beetham wearing white hat, c. 1896.

Reproduced with permission from the Wairarapa Archive in Masterton.

Vines sprout in Masterton

By 1882, William Beetham Jr could justifiably claim to have made good. For twenty years, he and his equally energetic brothers had worked hard, first to accumulate the deposit to help their father buy a block of land, and then even harder to break it in.

By 1860, when the family first arrived, the relatively open Wairarapa plains were largely settled or at least occupied by earlier arrivals like Dan Riddiford, or smallholders clustered around the embryonic towns of Masterton, Carterton, Greytown and Featherston. The Beethams had to go farther afield and in 1857 established what became the vast Brancepeth Station in the broken country north-east of Masterton. Not blessed with inherited wealth, William nevertheless became a man of substance and taste, and eventually commanded considerable mana in the infant community.

Returning from a visit to Britain in 1882, he travelled to Picardy, France. There he met and married Marie Zelie Hermanze Frere of Mereuil. Her Gallic allure captured his heart, then informed his palate, and within a year of their nuptials, Beetham had planted a tiny vineyard of Picardy cuttings at Towcett, his town house in Perry Street, Masterton.

Beetham made his first wine in 1887. Hermanze was perhaps the supervising winemaker. Certainly she was reported as the driving force behind the enterprise. At her instigation, Beetham later planted a larger vineyard of twelve varieties – including Pinot Noir, Pinot Meunier and Hermitage – at his other home, Lansdowne. Not surprisingly, given his wife's roots, Beetham aimed to make Burgundian and Bordeaux style wines, quite unlike the ports and sherries imported by the nascent local aristocracy. Mimicking those fortified classics were the sweet, strong wines produced and drunk at the time, by the Continental wine-bibbers at the other end of the colony's social ladder.

William Beetham with his wife Marie Zelie Harmanze Frere.

Reproduced with permission from the Wairarapa Archive in Masterton.

The first crop from Lansdowne in 1893 weighed 873 kilograms, and for a time thereafter production increased. But Beetham didn't regard his vineyard as a commercial enterprise, at least until some years later. In 1897, when Lansdowne produced 13.5 tonnes of grapes to make nearly 8,500 litres of wine, the *Wairarapa Times Age* described wine-making as "Mr William H. Beetham's hobby". Employing dozens of pickers, bird scarers and pruners to produce a small wine lake, is a redoubtable recreation indeed, but his lack of mercantile focus is not so surprising. Beetham's social position undoubtedly placed considerable entertainment demands on his cellar. Having his own supply must have saved a small fortune.

But Brancepeth already provided a good living. Peddling the odd bottle for a shilling or two, may have made no more sense than selling spare vegetables from the kitchen garden. In any case, demand for wine, particularly light-bodied (unfortified) wine, was low. The only people who preferred clarets and hocks, as they were known then, could probably afford to import the real thing. Or they had the means to grow their own. Indeed, Beetham's example was followed by several business associates, relatives and friends. J. N. Williams in Hastings, Bernard Chambers at Te Mata Station, Havelock North, and Henry Tiffen at Taradale, all established serious grape plantings.

Romeo Bragato, the Victorian government viticulturist who had such a profound subsequent effect on New Zealand's wine industry, visited Lansdowne in 1895, and on tasting the six-year-old Hermitage (Syrah/ Shiraz), pronounced the Wairarapa, great wine country.

Brancepeth 2002

Ed Beetham, William Beetham's great nephew, leads us down the long, narrow stairs beneath the gracious Brancepeth homestead. The home is immaculately preserved but these steps are seldom trod. Dishevelled boxes jumble the floor of the wine cellar, with a disparate assortment of bottles: dusty and empty. The four walls are lined with sturdy timber shelves, and stacked on them behind stout wire mesh 'earthquake' frames, is some of the oldest New Zealand-produced wine still in existence. 1898 Claret nestles next to Lansdowne Hock. Labels, on the few bottles that have them, tell us little except perhaps the date the cork was waxed: 1909 and 1917. Waxing is a considerable effort. Clearly these wines were expected to age. And have they stood the test of time? We might never have found out. You don't pull the cork on 100 year old wine for every casual visitor. But as Ed eases aside a wire frame to examine a label, it catches a protruding neck and sends the bottle tumbling to a shattering demise on the concrete floor. Oblivious to the shards, eager fingers dip into the spreading crimson pool, and are licked tentatively. There's not enough to pass formal judgement, but the wine is still robust and intact so far as we can tell. The opportunity to enjoy a very old wine can be brief.

Ed Beetham: 'Wyatt Creech came over one day with John Buck, John Comerford and Geoff Kelly. They were all excited about it. I did the classic thing and pulled the cork out of one bottle before they arrived so it would have plenty of time to breathe. By the time they got here it was pure vinegar. So we got another one, and John said, "Just leave it a tic … Now!" literally. And it was absolutely perfect. We poured a little into a tasting glass as soon as we'd pulled the cork out, and we tasted it. Not much good. By the time it went round again it tasted great. When it went round again it had gone.

'Subsequently Geoff wrote a great article for *National Business Review*. "Lansdowne's rosy glow lasts 80 years. The wine's still alive."'

Tararua

Just a year after Lansdowne's bumper 8,500 litre vintage, investor Capt A. Turner planted Tararua Vineyard, mainly in Pinot Noir, in Solway Street, at the southern end of Masterton. Tararua was a commercial enterprise from day one, and two years later in 1900, Turner employed bank clerk William Lamb, then only 20, as manager. Within four more years Lamb, obviously a quick learner, became sole owner and expanded the planting. He built a ventilated and sawdust-insulated winery, a fermenting house and a cellar. Business seemed promising for Tararua. Thirty boys were employed to pick the grapes for the 1906 harvest which produced nearly 4,500 litres of wine.

William Beetham began testing the market too, and from 1900 he also sold wine. In May 1905, the *Wairarapa Times Age* cited the two Masterton vineyards as exemplars for the government's encouragement of the 'new' wine industry. The future looked promising for the region's vineyards.

But Lamb's apparent success was transient. In 1908 the burgeoning Prohibitionist lobby scored its first victories in wine districts. Masterton and Eden in Auckland went 'dry'. To test the new laws, Lamb was charged – at his own request – with selling and keeping wine for sale within a no-license area. His defence rested on an apparent conflict in the law, and he was acquitted. The police appeal however, was heard before Chief Justice and avowed prohibitionist, Sir Robert Stout, who promptly overturned the acquittal and awarded seven guineas costs against Lamb. It's about here that history becomes murky. Most accounts hold that Stout's ruling made it an offence to grow (not just sell) wine in a no-license area. So Lamb's vineyard, being within Masterton's boundaries, had to go. Lamb's vines were certainly torn out, but shortly thereafter a group of Hawkes Bay vineyard owners reportedly challenged the decision by appealing for

Pam Ryan

'One of them went through their vineyard and marked the vines from which I should take the cuttings. I thought that was a very generous gesture.' Eric Bloomfield

clarification, and it was found to be in error, albeit too late for Lamb.

A closer reading of Stout's judgement however, contradicts some of this version. It appears all Lamb had to do was store and sell his wine across the Waingawa River. At around the same time, on advice from the Crown Law Office, winemakers in Henderson simply sold their wine from across the border of the next 'wet' area.

The mystery deepens further when we bring Beetham back into the frame. His vines at Lansdowne had also gone by this time. Tradition holds that Lansdowne's vines were ripped out at the same time as Tararua's, and for the same reason: Prohibition. But valuation records make no mention of Lansdowne as a vineyard after 1905, a full three years before the prohibitionist victory. In that year, Beetham's business affairs were reorganised, and a long-standing partnership ended. Perhaps the vineyard simply proved too demanding a 'hobby'. Whatever the cause, the Beethams paid Lamb five shillings a gallon for his remaining stock of claret, when Tararua's vines came out.

Phylloxera

Why would Lansdowne, so full of early promise, have been abandoned? Phylloxera, a small parasitic louse, endemic to the roots of American vines, is a possibility. It was unwittingly taken to Europe on vine rootstock around 1860, and over the next thirty years completely decimated European vineyards and reduced harvests catastrophically. Left to run its course, phylloxera eventually kills its hosts. Various counter-measures were tried, but only grafting European vines onto resistant American rootstock proved effective, and allowed the European industry to recover.

On his visit here in 1895, Romeo Bragato identified phylloxera, and in 1897 Agriculture Department officials discovered the pest at two small vineyards in Masterton. The treatment was drastic, invariably fatal for the vines, and from the sound of it, parlous to pretty much everything else in close proximity. The vines were ripped out, and remaining stumps treated with liberal dosings of kerosene. Bisulphide of carbon was then injected into the soil, just in case any of the little blighters had escaped. Lansdowne was inspected in 1897 and found to be clean, though declining tonnages over subsequent years could render that pronouncement suspect.

It wasn't until 1901, when Bragato was enticed back to New Zealand as government viticulturist, that effective measures were established. Grafted rootstock proved the only guarantee of immunity.

A Vine-free Zone

Prohibition scored body blows on the Wairarapa's and New Zealand's early wine industry. Rampant wowserism stigmatised demand and put more and more legal hobbles on winemakers and vintners. Masterton didn't go 'wet' again until 1946.

However the fundamental reason for the short lives of Wairarapa's two pioneer vineyards, after such a good start, may have been somewhat simpler. Business wasn't great. Beetham started selling wine in 1900, but his vines were pulled out within five years. Lamb could have tried to sell his wine outside Masterton. He apparently chose not to, but did continue to grow table grapes for some years. Perhaps New Zealand wine drinkers – the few there were – just weren't ready to buy the quality, in the quantity, that Beetham and Lamb produced.

Less than thirty years after the first cuttings went in, they had all gone. By 1911, Wairarapa's wine industry was dead: torn out root and vine.

Vine Roots

New Zealand's wine business has long been dominated by names of Continental or Mediterranean origin, but it was actually kicked off by some of the earliest British arrivals.

Chaplain and missionary Samuel Marsden planted New Zealand's first grapevines at KeriKeri in the Bay of Islands in 1819, just five years after first setting foot in the country. Twenty years later, British Resident James Busby produced our first wine. As a youth, the Scottish Busby had studied viticulture in France, and vigorously pursued his interest in the Antipodes. The 'father of Australian viticulture' brought Australian cuttings across the Tasman, and made his first vintage here in 1836. By 1840, when Busby's home became famous as the Treaty of Waitangi signing venue, several

gardens in the area boasted wine-producing vines.

In that same year, French settlers disembarked at Akaroa on Banks Peninsula, and grapes soon went in. Through the 1840s and '50s, more French, this time Marist priests, planted wine grapes at their missions in the Hokianga, up the Wanganui River, in Poverty and Hawkes Bays and in Gisborne. On a clearing beside the Kaipara Harbour, Englishman Charles Levet and his 14-year-old son, started a wine-making operation that provided them a living for four decades; and Spaniard Joseph Soler set up a vineyard and winery at Wanganui in 1866. Back in the Hokianga, German settlers produced wine in the 1880s.

So the majority of viticulturists and winemakers in nineteenth-century New Zealand hailed from wine-making and drinking cultures. That continued into the twentieth century as Dalmations and Lebanese put down vine roots. For many decades, wine was the tipple of only the upper class and Continentals. Neither swam in the social mainstream. The vast bulk of early New Zealand settlers were of British stock; and working to middle class at that. Their traditional potations were beer and whisky.

Between the advent of Prohibition and the 1950s, New Zealand's wine scene was a parched landscape, redeemed by oases of intense endeavour by pioneers like Assid Abraham Corban, Stipan Jelich, Josip Babich, Friedrich Wohnsiedler, Andrew Fistonich and Ivan Yukich. They are remembered for the brands they founded: Corbans, Pleasant Valley, Babich, Waihirere, Villa Maria, and Montana, but with a few exceptions the wine produced ranged from diabolical to mediocre.

Offshore investment from McWilliams in Hawkes Bay in 1947, the massive expansion of Gisborne's plantings in the late 1960s, and Montana's move into virgin territory in Marlborough in 1973, shifted the viticultural epicentre south from Auckland and re-forged the industry. Quality inexorably rose, though top wine couldn't be produced from the mostly hybrid grapes planted.

From the early sixties, licensing laws, which for decades had piously conspired against a sensible appreciation of wine (especially with food) began to relax. Drinking horizons broadened and accelerated the demand for change.

Pam Ryan

'Wine'arapa reborn

Martinborough

Throughout the ferment of vineyard expansion in the sixties and seventies, the Wairarapa slumbered, a traditional farming region of sheep and service towns over the hill from Wellington, its vineyard past a barely remembered interlude. Nowhere was more dyed-in-the-dusty-wool pastoral than Martinborough, some 50 kilometres by road south of Masterton.

The town had been laid out in the shape of the Union Jack by (and named after) John Martin, and the streets named for notable places Martin had visited, like Cologne and New York. By the 1970s, roading and communications had improved. The back country sheep stations the town serviced weren't so isolated, and Martinborough's importance as a service town had shrunk. It had become a fading township of dilapidated cottages settling into dusty anonymity on a road to nowhere. Apart from a couple of old European guys who'd had a few backyard vines, wine was not something you'd dream of associating with it. But it was here of all places, that the 1980s' oenological spotlight focussed with remarkable suddenness and intensity.

Within a decade, the area's wines would carry off a treasure chest of prizes, and Martinborough would eventually excel in more varieties than any other area of the country. With less than four per cent of the nation's vines, the Wairarapa punched above its weight from day one.

If Martinborough had no wine heritage, then the pioneer viniculturists cum winemakers who set up there were the perfect match. None had any commercial or professional background in the wine industry, and with one exception, precious little in the way of financial resources to see them through the first ravenous years of vineyard development.

The spectacle of normally prudent people throwing themselves and

their limited means into a fickle enterprise they knew next to nothing about
– planting classic grapevines on desiccated, stony paddocks – seemed at
the time the epitome of folly: an infectious but incurable lunacy. It was an
enormous leap of faith, though not completely blind. It was founded on
climate statistics and soil maps, if rather little capital.

Well, mostly. There was one harbinger of what was to come, though
no-one took much notice of him: a seventies prelude to the symphony of
viticultural endeavour of the 1980s. In 1973, Alister Taylor, famous (or
notorious) at the time as publisher of *The Little Red School Book* and Tim
Shadbolt's *Bullshit and Jellybeans*, rode into town in a borrowed Morris Minor
looking for land. He found 'a rundown orchard in a tiny, intensely hot
valley on the edge of Martinborough with an expanse of rusted roofs like
an old pa' and bought the package.

Alister Taylor: 'The local community thought we were mad. Martinborough at that stage was peopled by a mix of retards, ex-Maori slaves
and self-styled rural aristocracy. Sometimes the categories overlapped.
Opinion was that traditional rural activities should be continued. Even
the mayor was initially against vineyards, though he ended up taking
credit for later developments.

'I was brought up in Blenheim, and the area [Martinborough] re-
minded me of there: hot and dry. Neil McCallum and his mates did
soil surveys and enthused about how much like Bordeaux the soil was.
We had already figured that out by intuition.'

On gut instinct and bloody-mindedness, Taylor planted eight hectares
of vines in 1977–78: Chenin Blanc, Gewürtztraminer, Chardonnay and
Cabernet Sauvignon, among others, 'to see what would do best'.

Pretty soon the going got tough.

'We were ambitious and started to build a winery, but the architects
and Tim Shadbolt as the concrete contractor burned through a heap of
money and we still had nothing to show for it.'

Taylor bought more land and experimented with other crops. But despite, or perhaps because of, his range of ventures, his vineyard was
doomed. A combination of El Nino, rabbits, overweening optimism and
eventually debt, brought the dream tumbling down. Taylor was sold up

and left the area in 1983, just as the first plantings of Dry River, Chifney Wines, Ata Rangi and Martinborough Vineyard were poised to come on stream. His hunch about the land proved prescient nonetheless. The property at the end of Puruatanga Road was bought by Tom and Robin Draper, and was soon reborn as Te Kairanga.

Taylor's connection with Martinborough's wine wasn't completely severed. He subsequently ran a restaurant in the Bay of Islands, and the very first wine on its wine list was Ata Rangi Célèbre.

The olive and the grape.

Pam Ryan

Within just two years, four seminal Martinborough vineyards were established: Dry River Wines first in 1979, followed closely by Chifney Wines, Ata Rangi and Martinborough Vineyards the following year. Te Kairanga Wines joined the club in 1984. Why, some 70 years after Lamb and Beetham had jacked it in, did half a dozen people from totally different backgrounds, none in wine, all decide at virtually the same time, that the Wairarapa was the vinous Eldorado of New Zealand, and why in Martinborough?

The Wellington Incubator

As the nation's capital city, Wellington hosts most foreign embassies and consulates, and the head offices of a good many companies. Cosmopolitan professionals, diplomats, bureaucrats and corporates are thick on the ground. As a consequence, fine wine has never been a complete stranger in the city. If anywhere in the country were to sprout a circle of wine aficionados, Wellington would be that place. In the early 1970s, Wellington sprouted several wine-tasting groups, attended by names from the subsequent 'Who's Who' of New Zealand wine. Danny Schuster, winemaker, writer, researcher, teacher and all-round wine guru, took over a trade tasting group soon after starting at Avalon Wine and Spirits, then the leading wine shop in Wellington.

Derek Milne – Martinborough Vineyard: 'It was a wine-tasting group made up of people who became quite well known in later years. John Comerford, Geoff Kelly, Neil McCallum came in. Rumble came in, Brett Newell. Russell [Schultz] came in later years. That wine-tasting group was the most rigorous I've ever taken part in. It was always blind tasting. We did all the wines of the world. It was absolutely fascinating. That private group went right through from 1972, changing like George Washington's axe, probably into the early 80s.'

Neil McCallum – Dry River Wines: 'When Danny Schuster came to New Zealand, he had a wonderful cellar, and we did a lot of very interesting tastings in this funny little basement he'd dug out under the house he rented. I don't know how the house stayed up. Danny embedded my whole attitude to wine in concrete.'

Tom Draper – Te Kairanga Wines: 'John Buck was running wine appreciation courses and I went along and became good friends with him. Together we started the Magnum Society. John was first president and I was second. It was the first wine appreciation group without commercial affiliations, and became a nursery if you like, for a lot of people who became prominent in wines.'

Rosemary Chifney – Chifney Wines: 'When we came to New Zealand, Stan [Chifney] palled up with a pharmicist from Upper Hutt: Russell Schultz. He and Stanley went to Wellington once a week for twelve or fifteen weeks to a WEA wine appreciation course.'

Bonds were forged, connections made, loyalties cemented.

Derek Milne – Martinborough Vineyard: 'Even the ones who for various reasons (John Comerford wanted to devote his energies to judging and didn't want a conflict of interest) didn't want to invest in vineyards,

Pam Ryan

remained very strong supporters of those of us who did. Geoff Kelly wrote us up in NBR, and it was he in the very early days when there were only a few grapes planted, who really gave people faith that we were producing superb fruit.'

Derek Milne

In the mid 1970s Dr Derek Milne was an ambitious young government soil scientist with a deep and intensifying interest in wine: a passion nurtured by attendance at Danny Schuster's tastings. As one enthusiasm increasingly informed the other, Derek became intrigued by why various countries and particular regions within them, had specialised – sometimes for centuries – in the same kinds of wine.

Derek Milne: 'It fascinated me as to why the various little regions throughout Europe, grew the particular grapes and made the style of wine from those grapes, that they did, and had sometimes for hundreds of years. I wanted to investigate the climadaphic drivers that caused them to produce the particular raw material they did, to make their wine.

'By 1977 I was beginning to think we [in New Zealand] were growing grapes in areas that were too wet, particularly in the autumn. By that stage it started to become clear that there were certain technical climate parameters which were important. I'd worked out that if an area had more than one chance in five of more than 740 millimetres of rain per year, it was probably not a very suitable grape area, because you needed a dry autumn. Then my boss asked me to talk at the next Wine Institute meeting. I presented these ideas, to the stoniest silence you'd ever heard. At the time, Gisborne was being pushed as carrying New Zealand's wine future, and I was implying that despite being a good warm area, it would have difficulties in autumn in many years. With its good fertile soils, my figures showed Gisborne was probably going to be more suited to bulk wine, than to the greatest of New Zealand wines. Marlborough was still in its infancy then and there was huge optimism in Gisborne. My speech was like farting in the kitchen.

'From then on I just crunched numbers, and did a viticulture bulletin in 1978 showing where in New Zealand you would find the dry autumn areas. We were also starting to form an opinion about how much heat you needed to ripen the classic varieties: Riesling, Chardonnay, Cabernet Sauvignon and Pinot Noir. Basically we were trying to find the climate and the conditions that mimic the great wine growing regions.

'By '78 or '79 I had a model, where I'd taken twenty years of vintages in Bordeaux, Burgundy and Rheingau. I'd plotted heat days, rain-fall by month and classified the vintages into good, average and poor, then looked for patterns. And I got them. It is a matter of where the grape has the heat to ripen, in relation to the rainfall coming late in autumn or early winter. That was as crude as all hell. But it was enough. Martinborough is most like Dijon in northern Burgundy.'

Thirty years on, Derek still exudes intense excitement as he explains the graphs he developed from the great European wine regions as a young man. They gave him the confidence to pursue a dream of planting his own vines, in the only place close enough to his Wellington home to be practical: the Wairarapa.

Derek Milne: 'I wouldn't personally have chosen Martinborough over Blenheim or Hawkes Bay at that stage, but none of us could work out how we could manage any sort of viticultural operation in either of those places, whereas we had a chance in Martinborough. It was a question of looking for the very best local area.'

'We had to work outside and couldn't get it to ferment because of the cold. Stanley suggested they light a fire underneath. They did, and it worked.

Rosemary Chifney

Martinborough moves

While Derek and some of his fellow scientists were looking at Martinborough, Martinborough was beginning to look back. The town patently needed an economic shot in the arm. In 1979, Mayor Dawson Wright chaired a meeting in the town hall.

Pamela Bloomfield – Bloomfields Vineyard: 'They had real concerns about the area being depressed. Nothing had been planned for small areas of land now becoming available for development: land that was not particularly fertile. Years before, a market gardener, Mr Wong, had advocated growing cherries and grapes down Puruatanga Road, but getting access to that land seemed to be a problem.'

Duncan Milne – Martinborough Vineyard: 'The local mayor was trying to encourage horticulture in the area. They heard about Derek's report, and they invited him over to some sort of horticultural seminar at the town hall.'

Derek Milne – Martinborough Vineyard: 'The problem with that seminar was that you had all these conventional horticultural advisers standing up and saying if only you could get water here you could grow peaches, and whatever else. While I sat there completely bewildered and thought, "This is one of the driest areas in the North Island. It's suitable for dry climate crops. Why on earth are we trying to turn it into a wet climate area?"

'Not one person at this seminar was talking about olives, grapes, or herbs.'

That meeting was crucial in maturing the resolve of several of those present. Clive Paton (Ata Rangi) Wyatt Creech (Martinborough Vineyards and later Palliser Estate) and Neil McCallum (Dry River Wines), had already concluded that wine had a future in Martinborough.

Clive Paton – Ata Rangi: 'I attended the seminar on horticultural possibilities in the Martinborough area, then bought a four hectare block the same day I saw it.'

First Wines – The Gang of Four

Dry River Wines

The grand dinner of the 2002 Central Otago Pinot Noir Celebration is in full swing. It's mid-evening: between entrée and main. Diners are mingling, swapping notes on wines and sampling the offerings on other tables. Guests have been invited to bring a favourite bottle, and these stand four or five deep to the side of the main bar, available to everyone. Tom Pinckney reappears at our table radiating a mix of incredulity and rapture, and clutching a magnum of Dry River Pinot Noir. It must have been hidden behind the front bottles, he reckons. Within seconds half a dozen imploring pinotphiles, glasses extended, surround him. It's the find of the night.

In its relatively short life, Dry River has achieved a stature second to none in the New Zealand wine scene. Each vintage sells out within weeks at the highest average prices in the country. Pre-eminent wine writer and judge, Michael Cooper, gives the label the nod for five New Zealand Super Classics: Pinot Noir, Gewürztraminer, Pinot Gris, Riesling, and Botrytis Bunch Selection Gewürztraminer and Riesling. Super Classics are wines Cooper rates consistently brilliant over at least five vintages. Five from fewer than twenty is not a bad strike rate.

Formerly a researcher in organic chemistry, Dr Neil McCallum *is* Dry River. Neil applied his trademark intellectual rigour to Martinborough's prospects, and in 1979, guided by Derek Milne (with whom he worked) bought his block of land. Sourcing the best rootstock available, he started with Pinot Gris, Sauvignon Blanc and Gewürztraminer. He simply aimed to be the best, and quickly made a name for distinctive, bone-dry, long-cellaring whites.

Neil McCallum: 'Riesling was my very first love. I was a teetotaller until

Pam Ryan

Dr Neil McCallum. *Pam Ryan*

I was in my twenties, but in Oxford colleges they have extremely good chefs and superb cellars, and every week we'd have a special dinner. Our chef was rated the seventh best in Britain at that stage, and one night he served trout with an Oppenheimer Riesling. It was just magic. That's what did it for me: that one wine.'

Years later, having decided to switch from research to wine-making, Neil went into the scientific library and read every research paper in English on the subject. From there he decided on his starting point.

Neil McCallum: 'Wine-making is just like organic chemistry. You start from a theoretical point and you say "I want to end up with this particular practical result". The scientific method is linking the practical result to the intellectual idea. I came in [to wine-making] with a particular approach which is focussed on all the details, and then tried to translate all those accurately. If you are an organic chemist, you have a piece of paper in front of you saying the details are this, this and this; and if you get any of the variables wrong, you are screwed.'

Neil's devotion to detail is legendary. Ask commentators and other winemakers about him and you'll hear terms like 'uncompromising', 'pedantic', 'exacting', even 'Lenin-like fanatic'. The 'Good Doctor' as he's also known, wouldn't argue.

Neil McCallum: 'Winemakers are obsessional people, and I'm a very obsessional winemaker.'

And committed. For nearly ten years, Neil remained at his research job in Wellington, commuting across the Rimutakas at weekends to tend his vines. Then in 1988, disenchanted with government research policy and increasingly confident about his vineyard's future, Neil made the leap and wine became even more than an obsession. It became a full-time job as well. But while not a precarious existence, it was hardly a goldmine. Neil's insistence on doing things his way saw to that.

Neil McCallum: 'The big wineries have the economies of scale, but I don't think they get the pleasure out of it. I totally make the wines I want to make. There is no compromise. Every wine I make is the very best that I can do: at all stages from the vine growing right through to the wine-making. And everything we make is farmed by us. In big wineries the majority of wines are price point decisions. They play safe. My attitude is, if it's not right I won't do it.'

Neil initially didn't plant Pinot Noir, unsure whether it suited the area. In any case, his intensively self-taught wine-making skills were possibly better suited to whites in his early days. At its best, red wine-making is a light-handed operation, relying on the vineyard for top quality fruit. White wines are more in the hands of the winemaker. But once his confidence and skill in the vineyard grew, Neil produced Pinot Noir that's been compared to traditional fine Burgundy: tannic and somewhat unapproachable in its youth, with dense flavours and potential to drink elegantly for many years.

Dry River Wines

Neil doesn't make duds. If it has Dry River on the label, it will be good. Most of Dry River's production is sold by mail order, with about 15 per cent sold internationally, mainly in Britain. Since the mailing list is usually full, it can be extremely difficult to buy Dry River wine.

But wine of Dry River's stature is not made in a test-tube, and Neil acknowledges that scientific method is only the means to his artistic ends.

Neil McCallum: 'At the end of the day I still have to be able to look at a wine, have a good palate, and say, "This is the whole: the totality". And I think about whether it lacks or contains what I want artistically. The trick for me then is to be able to analyse it in my brain. That's the key point: the combination of artistic perception at one end, but at the other, being able to dissect, and then make the intellectual leap back to the variables where that perception comes from.'

Neil's individualistic approach combines deeply revered traditions and fastidiously researched innovation. It's not part of the man's nature to follow trends or to produce a wine or style because it's popular.

Neil McCallum: 'We choose the varieties we chose because I like the wines. You have to stand apart from fashion and concentrate on what are accepted quality standards. Most of our wine styles are different. I haven't had any regard for the public or what they want. A vineyard can be a taste leader. We are after something stand-out, and our wines are made to improve in the bottle rather than make an immediate impact.

'There is a stronger and stronger reaction against mass production: an anti-globalisation movement. People more and more want regional products, identifying with regional cultures. I hate the McDonalds movement. What I want is something very individual, matched to me. It's comparable to the Arts and Crafts Movement of the nineteenth century: hands-on with a rigorous intellectual framework. But it's an artistic, cultural movement at heart.'

In 2003, Neil sold Dry River Wines to Americans Reg Oliver and Julia Robertson, but he remains chief winemaker. How long does he see himself staying?

Neil McCallum: 'For as long as it's mutually acceptable, which I imagine will be many years.'

Chifney Wines

Sadly, Stan Chifney is no longer with us, but you gain some measure of the man from the photo in Martinborough's Wine Centre of Stan playing his violin among his grapevines. His wines, slowly maturing in oak in his cellar, apparently received the same melodious attention.

Stan's impact on the infant Martinborough wine scene was seminal. Originally from England, Stan and his wife Rosemary spent many years in West Africa and the Middle East where Stan, with his microbiology training, produced vaccines and established laboratories. They moved to New Zealand for a job at ICI's Tasman Vaccine division in Upper Hutt.

As a boy, Stan had made ginger beer, then fruit wines. In the Hutt, he explored the real thing. For several vintages, he and Russell Schultz, later of Martinborough Vineyards, drove to Napier to pick grapes. There was always a grower or two who would let them buy a trailer load. Plastic rubbish bags of fruit were loaded on the trailer, driven back to the Hutt, and trod in Russell's garage. The pair split the juice and each made his own wine: always red, and mostly Cabernet.

Then Tasman changed hands and Stan, just two years from compulsory retirement, decided to jump early.

Rosemary Chifney: 'We'd been to Australia on a holiday to see our oldest daughter, and visited vineyards in the Hunter Valley. When we left she gave us a book called *How to Start Your Own Vineyard.* A little while later Stan announced whilst drying the dishes one night, "I think we'll start a vineyard." Little did I realise what we were letting ourselves in for: a lot of hard work.'

Having heard about the horticultural seminar in Martinborough, Stan and Rosemary obtained one of the very last copies of the council's report. They also heard there was land for sale. Not wanting to limit their options, they caravanned through Martinborough, Hawkes Bay and Gisborne looking for suitable sites. But the further north they went, the more difficult to find – and expensive – land became. They quickly settled on Martinborough and bought their plot in July 1980. Later that year, the Chifneys bought a house in New York Street for their daughter and her family returning from Australia. A Mr Lou Szabo had grown grapes and made wine for personal consumption on that plot only a few years before.

But what to plant? Martinborough had no wine pedigree to refer to. Darling of the time was Müller Thurgau, still being copiously planted in Gisborne and Hawkes Bay. But the writing was on the vineyard wall, as Derek Milne had predicted. A wine glut was looming, and in 1987 Müller Thurgau would be the main cause and casualty of the government subsidised vine pull. In any case, Stan was a Cabernet man. He did plant Chenin Blanc, Chardonnay and Gewürztraminer, but two thirds of his vines were the red Bordeaux varieties Cabernet Sauvignon, Cabernet Franc and Merlot. The 1984 Chenin Blanc was Stan's very first wine, and it drew some dedicated customers from then on. His first competition entry in 1986, was the 1985 Cab Sav. It won gold from a judging panel that included Jancis Robinson, the doyen of wine scribes and broadcasters. Chuffed as he was, Stan's ultimate ambition was to drink his own ten-year-old Cabernet Sauvignon. He exceeded that goal by a year, and annually thereafter, a glass has been poured on his grave.

The Chifney's winery, built in 1983 with a partly subterranean cellar, was the only one in Martinborough for the first few years. Everyone's wine was made there.

Duncan Milne – Martinborough Vineyards: 'The first year we produced wine was 1984. We all sat around before that and said "Well, who's going to build a winery? Who's going to get some tanks or something?" We hadn't thought that through. Stan said "Well I'm building a winery anyway, before I drop off the perch and miss out." We owned a few tanks so we moved them into Stan's winery, and all made our wine in there sort of cooperatively and Stan kept an eye on it. I think we used Stan's basket press. Russell Schultz basically made our wine. Stan had a bit of a lab. That was the first year.'

Rosemary Chifney: 'Clive's [Ata Rangi] first Pinot Noir got the first gold in the area. We had to work outside and couldn't get it to ferment because of the cold. Stanley suggested they light a fire underneath. They did, and it worked. Another winemaker wrapped electric blankets around the tanks to get his Cabernet Sauvignon going. It was fun but your hands were shaking.'

Stan's wines, said by one commentator to 'reflect the man himself – full of personality, idiosyncratic and capable of long aging', continued to win

The late Stan Chifney. *Pam Ryan*

prizes. Against growing opinion in the area, he contended that Burgundian and Bordeaux varieties could both be grown successfully. So firm was his preference for Bordeaux reds, that when Clive Paton gave him some Pinot Noir vines, he planted them along the road to keep the dust off the Cabernet Sauvignon. Then in 1991 he threw their fruit into his Garden of Eden red, along with Cabernet Sauvignon, Gamay, Pinot Meunier and Cabernet Franc.

Stan Chifney: 'I mixed Bordeaux and Burgundy – a cardinal sin – and I got a gold medal for it. I think the judges were confused.'

Stan died in 1996, and his daughter Susan, who had worked alongside him from the beginning, stepped up to the mark to take over the vineyard and winery. In 2000, Rosemary and Susan decided to 'let go', selling to neighbouring Margrain Vineyard.

Rosemary Chifney: 'Looking back, I do feel that all the effort *was* worthwhile. Even so, none of us really envisaged the huge growth in and around the town. Well may it continue.'

Ata Rangi

Clive Paton, patriarch of the Ata Rangi whanau, has dinner guests, but he finishes his meal, as always, with red wine and bread. It's been a typical day for Clive. After delivering his youngest daughter to the early school bus, he was in the winery before eight. Half his morning was taken up digging out tenacious but poorly performing Sangiovese vines to make way for more Pinot Noir. He then hosted a local vintners' meeting trying to thrash out the local appellation dispute. Tasting with brother-in-law Olly Masters, Ata Rangi's other winemaker, to blend the Célèbre, wound up his day in the winery, before the school soccer team needed their coach in attendance. Just on dark he pedalled home from a cross-country mountain bike ride. A compact man of prodigious energy, he's learning to conserve it. The winery he worked so hard to establish, now runs like a clock, without his constant presence.

Blowers is being emptied for pressing. The tall stainless tanks at Ata Rangi have names rather than numbers. They're easier to remember. Henry Blofeld, whose passion for cricket almost equals his devotion to wine, visited the day after this one was commissioned. So Blowers it became. The free-run juice is drained first to make emptying easier. Later, it will be

Clive Paton, Ata Rangi. *Pam Ryan*

blended back with the pressed juice. Strong wafts of blackcurrant rise from the tank. Closer up these become savoury animal smells as if from a newly gutted animal. The fresh blood colour heightens the slaughterhouse impression.

Intact berries make up a proportion of the fruit that tumbles out after the juice. 'Little nuggets of flavour,' cellarman Grant Stanley calls them. They slow down the fermentation by holding back nutrients and making the yeast work harder. In fact they are fermenting inside, greatly reducing harsh malic acid and producing higher alcohol and glycerol, giving the wine a lovely, slightly slippery texture in the mouth. Carbonic maceration, as the process is called, also contributes flavourful aromatic compounds to the eventual wine.

Grant brings over a sample of nearly fermented Syrah for Clive to taste. He's concerned it might start to oxidise. Tasting it is like sticking your head in a pepper grinder, and the unfiltered juice is almost chewy in the mouth. Clive gives it just a little longer in the fermenting vat. It's a fine line.

Ata Rangi Wines

Ata Rangi's three great wines are Pinot Noir, Célèbre (A delicious Merlot/Cabernet Sauvignon/Syrah blend), and Craighall Chardonnay. Also produced is the fine, Chablis-like Petrie Chardonnay, barrel-fermented Sauvignon Blanc, Pinot Gris and a fun, refreshing Summer Rose.

Ata Rangi: Dawn Sky – a new beginning. For Clive, it was all that and more. Selling a herd of dairy cows to buy the land, he gave himself ten years to make a go of it. He hit the financial wall in two. On top of that, his irrigation was inadequate, shelter from the merciless Wairarapa winds was non-existent, and he knew next to nothing about grapes. He didn't have that on his own.

Clive Paton: 'When I started, there was no history here. I was aiming at something in my head. I didn't have anyone to emulate and there wasn't stuff on the ground to walk through. But you just go and do it. We were all in different situations, but it was new to all of us and we were all undercapitalised.'

Clive planted his first vines in 1980. His first vintage was 1985. To make ends meet in the meantime, he grew pumpkins and garlic, worked as a county ranger and even dug graves. It was a Herculean effort. In 1982 he had to bring in a financial partner. The same year, his sister Alison bought two hectares next door. She planted four rows of Gewürztraminer. That was the first, albeit unconscious, step towards Ata Rangi's current

The Ata Rangi team. From left
Alison, Clive, Phyll, Olly. *Pam Ryan*

partnership. The next followed when he met his wife, Phyll, then a
winemaker at Montana in Marlborough. In 1987, Phyll bought out the
partner. Ata Rangi's situation and achievements by 1990 far exceeded the
expectations Clive had held in 1980.

Phyll Pattie: 'But we still had no money and no income. Clive really was
living incredibly lean so I got an R&D job with the Dairy Board for two
years.

'We borrowed twenty thousand dollars from my parents to buy our
first press, a funny fibreglass thing. I also took on the business adminis-
tration, which I knew nothing about. Since there hadn't been much

income before, there hadn't been much need for that except for paying the bills, but Clive was never good at paperwork. I also took on the white wine-making. I made the Gewürz and the Chardonnay till '94, and helped with the red. I was strong on wine-making and record keeping, and set up a lab. But I knew nothing about growing grapes.'

Clive is naturally a grower rather than a technician. But he had acquired considerable wine-making skill working the 1981 and '82 vintages in a couple of Auckland wineries. Together he and Phyll formed a strong team that was reinforced further when Oliver Masters arrived in 1989, armed with biotech, viticulture and oenology degrees.

Olly worked for several vineyards and wineries in Martinborough, and was closely involved in the establishment of Margrain Vineyard. His future at Ata Rangi was cemented in 1991, however, when Alison returned after stints working in the wine trade in both Wellington and London. Love blossomed and in 1995 Ata Rangi was reconstituted as a foursome. That meant a reallocation of responsibilities.

Phyll Pattie: 'I loved wine-making and knew that the foursome would mean I'd lose it. I cried for an hour after the decision was made, but I was able to put my creative energies into marketing.'

A reformed Ata Rangi also meant the inevitable burdens of a smaller wine business could be spread.

Alison Paton: 'There aren't many industries where you are expected to grow it, make it, market it, finance it, be some sort of public guru and have a lifestyle. Having four of us, and the age spread between Clive and Olly, allows for future continuity at Ata Rangi and makes us a lot less vulnerable if one of us gets run over by a bus. Being a one person band in a small winery can be very insecure.'

By now, Phyll had something to market. The 1988, '89 and '90 Célèbres all won major awards. The Chardonnay was well on the way to becoming the superb world class wine it is today. But Ata Rangi's greatest expression is Pinot Noir. The '86 Pinot Noir won gold. The 1993 vintage won them the Bouchard-Finlayson Trophy from the UK's International Wine and Spirit Competition of 1995. This is one of the wine world's greatest prizes, and Ata Rangi Pinot Noir has won it three times. Clive is unequivocal – and modest. The trick is in the growing.

Clive Paton: 'If you know a vineyard plot over the years, and you know you're going to get consistent fruit, it makes it pretty easy. You can do a lot more with fantastic fruit: in terms of length of ferment, extraction levels, alcohol. The whole thing can be taken further, and it makes the whole job less problematic than saying "Am I going to get green-skinned tannins? I'll shorten the ferment, or am I going to get beetroot characters out of the 10-5 [clone]?"'

That wasn't just Ata Rangi that Clive steered in the right direction. Many later arrivals on the Martinborough wine scene appreciatively remember Clive's advice, assistance and support. So do his family.

Phyll Pattie: 'Just about every night of the week someone would be on the phone to Clive, wanting to know how to do it. It was crazy, really.'

Alison Paton: 'And we were constantly asked to make wine for other people. It's a real catch-22. You want to do a job well for somebody else. And so you get all this angst about their wine when you should be focussing on your own. And if you do a really good job, you're establishing their reputation for them in competition with your own. In the end, we decided it was too hard, and anyway, we simply didn't have the time, as the demands of our growing business and families escalated.'

After an incredibly straitened incubation period, Ata Rangi has fledged as a high-flier in the New Zealand wine firmament. There's no chance however, of the partnership slipping into cruise mode.

Oliver Masters: 'Things are always changing. There was no guarantee that the early choices were all the right ones. But the good winemakers are not doing the same things now that they were ten years ago. I notice how in tune with the industry some people are. Some are head in the sand doing their own thing, but others are going to tastings and technical conferences and workshops, and being in touch with changes. Twenty years seems like a century ago, and the standard keeps rising.'

Bird nets, Ata Rangi. *David Wall*

'When I started, there was no history here. I was aiming at something in my head. I didn't have anyone to emulate and there wasn't stuff on the ground to walk through. But you just go and do it.' Clive Paton

Martinborough Vineyard

Pam Ryan

Duncan Milne: 'I remember the very first meeting we had of our new partnership, and Derek brought along a bottle of Grand Cru Burgundy, and popped it on the table, pulled the cork and said, "This is the objective." There was no MBA business plan to make shit-loads of money. It wasn't a money thing. The objective was to produce great wine. If we do that, everything else will follow. And we all sipped the Burgundy in Wyatt's little shack.'

Martinborough Vineyard was born of a fortuitous combination of land, people and timing. The land, on Princess Street, belonged to Wyatt Creech. A Hawkes Bay friend from a South African vineyard family had mentioned to Wyatt, more than once, that Martinborough had potential for wine. That struck a chord. Wyatt's mother was a Beetham. So grapes were at the back of his mind when he bought the block in 1978 and planted vegetables.

In 1979, Stan Chifney's wine-making mate, Russell Schultz, was looking at planting his own vines too.

Russell Schultz: 'Neil [McCallum] had already bought land and my reaction was "You've got to be bloody joking!" Then Neil introduced me to Derek [Milne]. Sue and I went over and Jess Creech [Wyatt's land agent father] showed us around the area. Then he phoned up and said Wyatt would sell us some of his land. So I rang Derek to see if he wanted to be involved.'

Derek Milne: 'Russell said to me, I don't know anything about viticulture. I need someone to advise me. I just reacted instinctively and said I was happy to go in with him. It was almost one of those divine signs. Because Neil and other people had bought up land. I'd done all this technical work, yet I wasn't involved.

We drew a sensible boundary across Wyatt's land and it turned out to be sixteen acres which was more than we could afford. Wyatt said "I'm interested in coming in too." That made it affordable.'

Wyatt Creech: 'They were keen on establishing a vineyard and I said I'd come in with them, because I enjoyed living here and had equipment and was in a better position to do it.

I had high hopes for this. I thought it had plenty of potential, because wine was coming up everywhere in New Zealand at that stage and people were getting a lot more interested. I think our instincts turned out right.'

Duncan Milne: 'My wife Claire and I were living in America, when Derek was thinking about buying a bit of land. I said, "Let's do it, and try your theory out." We came back from the States about that time. That's how we started: Derek, Russell and Sue, Wyatt, and Claire and me.'

Russell Schultz: 'I became involved through ignorance.'

Derek Milne: 'We were doing what you do when you don't know what you are doing.'

Wyatt Creech: 'We had relatively scant knowledge, but as a collective we didn't have *no* knowledge about what we were trying to do. Russell had been making wine on an amateur basis. Derek had been involved

Martinborough Vineyard Wines

All Martinborough wines are impressive, but the flagship is Pinot Noir, and 70 per cent to 80 per cent of their planting will soon be in the princely red. The balance is in Chardonnay, Riesling and Pinot Gris. The Chardonnay is superb: oaky and fruity. The Pinot Gris ranks with the country's best. That leaves a deliciously rich botrytised Late Harvest Riesling to finish.

in wine-tasting groups. I had a much lower level of knowledge of that than him, but I had an agricultural and accounting background.

'Many of the decisions we made then turned out to be one thing drives another. Originally the idea was to plant just an acre or so a year and let the thing grow in a very slow and organic way. But that ended up being set by the wayside. When we decided to get cuttings we were going to get a lot so we planted them all. And once we had such a lot of grapes growing, we thought we might as well plant all of the land.'

The team found themselves on an accelerating conveyor, and as they committed ever more resources and time, they had to keep running faster, learning as they went. Luck played its part.

Derek Milne: 'Coming into the '85 crop, I still had some connections in the financial and political world. During the last days of Muldoon, a friend rang up and said, "Piggy's ruining the country. It's all going to turn to shit and there will be a massive devaluation." We'd been looking at bringing a press in from overseas. On the Thursday we decided we'd better do it now. On the Friday we bought Deutchmarks and TT'd them to Germany to buy this press. At three o'clock the money got through and at five o'clock the Forex markets were frozen and New Zealand went into limbo for three days. We thought we were pretty smart on the currency trading, but on the other hand we owned this sophisticated press in Germany, and we had no building, no winery, no tanks, no nothing. But away we went, had our winery built and bought some tanks and Russell and I made all the wine in '85. We moved in as the builders moved out: every time a builder moved a ladder we put a tank there.

'This press came all the way from Germany perfectly intact, and then on the truck from Auckland the truckie let it slide and crushed the whole control panel. Two or three days off needing it, we had no control panel and the instructions were in German. So we rang up the local electrician. He came around, pulled panels off, switched some wires around and fixed it up the opposite to the instructions. It's worked perfectly since. Then the insurance bought us a new control panel a year later. We couldn't work that out so we've never used it. It's still in the loft. Everyone knows how to use the old control panel and the local electrician knows how to fix it.'

Duncan Milne, Martinborough Vineyard. *Pam Ryan*

By 1984 however, Wyatt confronted a dilemma. He still owned a sizeable chunk of obviously promising land, which he also wanted to plant in vines. But the partnership needed a winery, and soon. Realising he didn't have sufficient capital to do both, Wyatt chose to go his own way and form another partnership: Om Santi. After additional expansion, and the involvement of more investors, Om Santi was eventually reincarnated in 1987 as Palliser Estate.

Martinborough Vineyard's partners clearly saw fine Pinot Noir as their Holy Grail from the start. But initially Gewürztraminer, Chardonnay, Malbec, Merlot, Chenin Blanc, Cabernet Sauvignon, Sauvignon Blanc and Durif were also planted. Yet it soon became obvious that their wine-making skills didn't match their aspirations.

Russell Schultz: 'I made the wine in '84 with small volumes. In '85 I made the wine again. But it became clear I didn't have the expertise, or the absolute dedication. I had a family I couldn't leave to devote everything to wine. John Hancock recommended Larry McKenna and we hired him.'

Australian Larry McKenna, the first trained wine professional in the Martinborough area, bought a share of the partnership. He liked what he found in the area, especially the Pinot Noir.

Larry McKenna: 'I tasted a few from the barrel, like Clive's at Ata Rangi, and they just blew me away. And they were from people who theoretically didn't know what they were doing! So that was a very good start for me. From a professional wine-making point of view, what was in the barrel was very, very good.'

Larry faced an enormous challenge to set Martinborough Vineyard; up until then run by enthusiastic part-timers; on a professional footing.

Larry McKenna: 'They had only just built the winery, and they'd bought all this stuff and just put it in there. It was hopeless. They were all trying to do it part-time. I spent a year getting it together. I threw out an enormous amount of junk. The vineyards were a bloody mess. They had field-grafted, and a lot had failed. There was no uniformity in the vineyard. Some very vigorous canopies had fruit inside going rotten. I had to throw a lot away.'

But there is no doubt the raw material was there, both in the fruit and the winemaker. Although he'd never made Pinot before, Larry's '86 Pinot Noir won gold. It was no fluke. Martinborough Vineyard went on to a straight run of golds in five consecutive vintages. Larry rapidly became a central pillar in Martinborough's Pinot temple of achievement.

Autumn blaze.   *Pam Ryan*

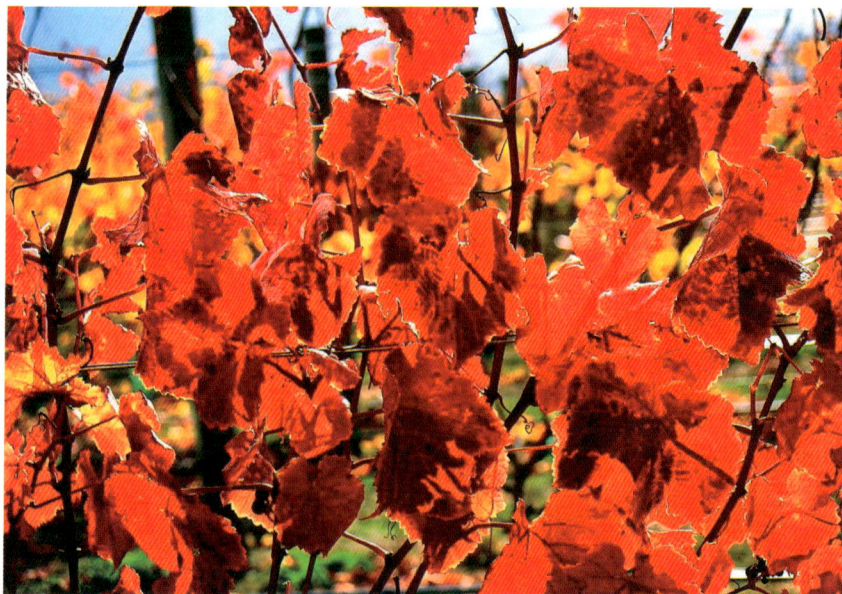

That run of spectacularly successful vintages accelerated the growth of the business, and increased the demands on the small team. From 1986 through 1988 Larry worked as winemaker only, but in 1989 he took over as CEO too. He did both jobs for nearly a decade, until 1998 when the roles were split and Duncan Milne took over as CEO while an outside replacement was found. After a further year as winemaker, Larry McKenna left Martinborough Vineyards. He is now developing his own vineyard: Escarpment, on Te Muna terrace, just south of Martinborough.

Appointed in 2000, new winemaker Claire Mulholland already had experience making quality Pinot Noir at Gibbston Valley in Central Otago. She is well aware of the weighty legacy she inherited.

Claire Mulholland: 'Martinborough Vineyard has a great name and Larry was a huge part of that. So to some extent it's daunting to follow in his footsteps. But I knew Larry from way back, and it's good to be able to talk to him.

'Within six years we'll crush one hundred tonnes of Pinot Noir. We have ten different clones, and several different rootstocks, all with different flowering times, and different cropping levels. We'll keep them all separate and blend for complexity. That will get very interesting. The philosophy of the company is to move towards concentrating on Pinot Noir, but the region does very well in Sauvignon Blanc, Chardonnay, Riesling and Pinot Gris too, so we intend to do everything really well.'

Sauvignon Blanc has been discarded, and Martinborough Vineyard produces superb examples of all the rest. Their supreme accomplishment was the 1997 Bouchard-Finlayson Trophy for Pinot Noir. Quality comes ahead of expansion. Having bought fruit from growers around the district for some time, Martinborough Vineyard now restricts its production to that distinct arc of land around the town known as the Martinborough Terrace. The partners know the fruit it produces. They know what they can do with it; and they still know where they want to be.

Derek Milne: 'You can make wine with all the technical expertise you like, but if you don't know what you are aiming for or can't recognise high style or whatever, you are never going to produce it. Burgundy is what we are aiming at.'

The Martinborough 'saucer'.

David Wall

'We were doing what you do when
you don't know what you are doing.'

Derek Milne

Masterton re-emerges

The Wairarapa wine renaissance wasn't confined to Martinborough, although it began and remains centred there. At Solway at the southern end of Masterton, only metres from where Lamb planted and then ripped out his Tararua vineyard so long ago, a new vineyard sprouted into life in 1982.

Bloomfields Vineyard

Eric and Pamela Bloomfield had enjoyed wine for years. Indeed their travels always seemed to lead them to the Loire or lower Rhone valleys. Back home in the Wairarapa, they had to make do with Bakano vintage comparisons. That was in the late sixties and early seventies.

Eric Bloomfield: 'We were living out at Te Ore Ore then, with a background of the little hills over there. There was a property on a delightful slope and I used to dream about planting a vineyard up there. But it wasn't really possible.

'Then I got hints of things starting to happen in Martinborough. So I went down there, and explored quite a lot. I was getting quite keen on the idea until I realised that I was going to do this after work and on weekends. And the practicalities from Masterton were just zilch.

'So I started a little hunt around here for what was available. Somebody put me onto a guy who worked with Derek Milne. He had access to all the information about soil types. We looked at various pieces of land and when this became available we checked it out and eventually bought it.'

Pamela Bloomfield: 'We were quite amazed really, because it was the most unglamorous piece of land. You have romantic notions of vineyards. You don't imagine it to be down by the [Waingawa] river with a whole lot of rubbish dumped on it. There was even a big dredge in the middle. But it had terribly arid, stony soil and a long, slow ripening period.'

Eric Bloomfield: 'I went to see Danny Schuster at Lincoln to find out where I could get cuttings. I got some from an orchard north of Christchurch for which Danny was the adviser. The other source was the Babich boys. They were utterly helpful and totally un-precious. I thought they had the most consistent Pinot Noir at the time, even though they were in Henderson. One of them went through their vineyard and marked the vines from which I should take the cuttings. I thought that was a very generous gesture.'

Most of those first vines planted at Bloomfields in 1982 were classic Bordeaux varieties: Cabernet Franc, Merlot, Cabernet Sauvignon and Sauvignon Blanc, as well as some Chardonnay and Pinot Noir. The rest of the ten acres was planted in 1987, a year after Pamela and Eric's son, David Bloomfield and his wife, Janet, returned from overseas and entered a partnership with Eric and Pamela.

With full-time attention, the vineyard progressed to new levels, and David, who had no background in wine except for attending Wellington wine society tastings, soon earned a reputation as passionate, innovative and capable of creating winery and vineyard equipment from whatever was at hand.

Within six years, a house was relocated from Wanganui as the vineyard homestead, an old butcher's shop from the Waingawa Abbatoirs became the bottling and packing room, and more land was purchased. By 1997, when the winery capacity reached 100 tonnes, the wine bug had infected David Bloomfield to his core. But the vineyard couldn't provide sufficient challenge and he sold up, to begin a post-graduate diploma in oenology at Lincoln University. That became a Masters, which in turn grew into a doctoral thesis focussing on tannins and phenols. David is completing that now.

The vineyard in Solway Crescent has had two owners since the family sold, and other plantings have subsequently been established around Masterton, but it was the Bloomfields who led the way. And it will be surprising if the New Zealand wine scene doesn't hear more from the younger Bloomfield in the future.

The Big Two

At either end of the crescent-shaped Martinborough Terrace, are the larger players on the Wairarapa vineyard scene: Te Kairanga and Pallliser. Both are public companies investing heavily to produce substantially rising volumes.

Te Kairanga Wines

Te Kairanga's splendid new winery seems deserted, as if everyone has gone home early, and forgotten to turn the music off. Yet behind the lyrical Bach Concerto is the perceptible murmur of industry: the occasional dull ring of steel on steel, the soft mush of plunging must. Along one wall of the designer concrete building, squats a row of dumpy stainless tanks topped by a wide catwalk. Through the centre, much taller tanks loom, gleaming toward the roof. A stack of taut new, oak barrels, bungs crammed into holes stained like children's mouths after raspberry drink, grows higher every day. A dozen fantails chase vinegar flies in twittering, swooping dog-fights. Straddling the yawning space like an over-muscled coat-hanger on rails, is a gantry crane, transfer pot slung idly beneath. There are no must pumps. Gallic voices echo, and Nicholas, a visiting French cellarhand, appears from behind some tanks he's cleaning, to help his compatriot Stephanie plunge a deep tank of Pinot Noir.

It's all a far cry from the vineyard's beginnings. Te Kairanga's first fruit was carted down to Chifneys' in washing baskets for Stan to deal with. After a couple of vintages, Te Kairanga's own winery was built, and Stan came to them. Earlier still, when Tom and Robin Draper bought Alister Taylor's over-mortgaged 200-acre property in 1984, it could hardly be called a vineyard.

Tom Draper: 'We got about five acres of little sticks in the ground. We

Te Kairanga Wine

Te Kairanga had some difficult years, but the company has worked hard and invested heavily to lift and maintain wine quality. That effort shows most in their superb Chardonnays and bold Reserve Pinot Noir, the varietals Peter Caldwell feels most affinity for. TK also make an oak-aged Sauvignon Blanc and from 2001 on a fine Riesling. Production is augmented with fruit from Gisborne and Hawkes Bay, to make Castlepoint and Gisborne Chardonnay.

had to brush aside the weeds to find them. The best of his [Taylor's] grapes were Gewürztraminer down on the flat, but it was too damp. We subsequently sold that land and those vines were pulled out. Up top there was Chardonnay planted but it all died. For all practical purposes we started afresh.'

Tom's interest in wine pre-dates Te Kairanga by decades.

Tom Draper: 'I got interested in wines from being exposed to them in the early days of licensed restaurants. Hardly anybody drank wine then. I used to buy wine from Mission and from Te Kauwhata Research Station. That's how John Buck got to know me. He had the wine shop in Johnsonville, and the Napier-Wellington transport truck used to pull in with four cases of wine for him and four for me. He used to wonder who this Tom Draper was.'

Tom rationalised the vineyard by selling off most of the 200 acres and keeping the portion that is present-day Te Kairanga. He reckons this remnant of John Martin's original farm is the best part of the Martinborough Terrace. The gravels are the deepest and freest draining, and the highest. The terrace drops twenty metres from here to the north-western end: frosts tend to roll off. A year after buying, Tom brought in shareholders, formed a partnership, and planted Chardonnay, Pinot Noir, Sauvignon Blanc and Cabernet Sauvignon.

Tom Draper: 'Martinborough was very cooperative in the early days, in everything except marketing. We borrowed each other's gear, and met on a regular basis to taste each other's wine.'

Te Kairanga's first decade was one of consolidation and learning: sometimes the hard way. The first winemaker in 1989 was less than successful and lasted barely a year. He was succeeded by Chris Buring, who worked seven vintages.

Chris Buring: 'There were only six producers in Martinborough then [1990]. I did a flying visit and was rapt with the flavours I found. That's why I've stayed ever since. Chardonnay, Sauvignon Blanc and Pinot Noir were all impressive in the '88 vintage.'

Consultant winemaker Brent Marris managed the difficult 1998 vintage: the culmination of a drought ridden season. He produced some fine wines, and left just a small batch of Cabernet Sauvignon to be finished by incoming winemaker Peter Caldwell.

The variety, planted originally on the back of Stan Chifney's early success, no longer fitted well in the TK range and was being progressively replaced. It didn't ripen as consistently as in other places; is difficult to market, especially straight Cabernet rather than blended with say Merlot; and the land was proving too good for Pinot Noir, to risk leaving in Cab Sav. Imagine the TK team's delight, tempered with slight embarrassment, when the 1998 Te Kairanga Cabernet Sauvignon won a gold medal and the trophy for best wine at the Air New Zealand wine awards.

In 1991, Te Kairanga had become a public company in order to fund accelerating growth. In 1993, Andrew Shackleton was appointed CEO. Andrew's love affair with wine started early.

Andrew Shackleton: 'As kids we were allowed a sherry glass of wine with dinner. My parents had learned about wine in the UK, and set up the Wine and Food Society in Dunedin. They tried to educate Dunedin society to get off spirits and cocktails and onto wine.'

To the CEO role, Andrew also brought farm and business management qualifications and twenty years' experience in the wine industry in France, London, Australia and New Zealand.

Managing both Te Kairanga's burgeoning supply, and its rapidly increasing demand, is one of Andrew's main challenges.

Andrew Shackleton: 'The bulk of our wine is sold on the domestic market. Thirty-five to forty per cent is allocated to export. We couldn't afford more [for export] while customers within New Zealand had to be looked after. But it's a tougher and tougher market here. There are more brands but static consumption. So the bulk of our new production will be aimed at export: mostly to the States, UK, Australia and Canada. And also to Asia.'

The third part of TK's big challenge is to maintain high quality as production and markets grow. The new winery was designed to expand to a thousand tonne capacity. That's nearly five times the current crush.

Peter and Mayi Caldwell,
Te Kairanga Estate. *Pam Ryan*

'In France the winemaker is responsible
for the vineyard. The vineyard is the key
to the quality of wine.' Peter Caldwell

Over the three years current winemaker Peter Caldwell worked in the
old, cramped winery, he reorganised the processes, making them gentler.
Out went all must pumps; small vat ferments were favoured and the winery
bought a pneumatic plunger. To maintain a gentler regime while aiming
at five times greater production demands considerable innovation. Peter
developed hydraulically tipped feeder bins, inspection conveyors, and
worm feeds that don't break up the fruit. The transfer pot replaces must
pumping. Filled in one part of the winery, the pot is hoisted aloft, craned
to the recipient tank, then lowered and emptied in.

Originally from Tasmania, Peter gained his wine-making qualifications
at Roseworthy, then worked throughout Australia and North America. He
met his wife Mayi, also a winemaker, in California. Mayi sparked Peter's
interest in working in her native Bordeaux. There, Peter redefined his wine-
making approach.

Peter Caldwell: 'I consciously brought attitudes I'd picked up in France
over here. I was absolutely amazed at what they did in France. It made
a lot of sense to me. It was what I wanted to do. I couldn't stand to be in
a place where you just produced tonnes and tonnes of whatever to a
recipe and a cost.

'In France the winemaker is responsible for the vineyard. The vineyard is the key to the quality of wine. So wine-making is very hands off, because the quality of the fruit has been determined already.

'We use the transfer pot. No must pumps. They can damage and aerate the must. I saw a transfer pot while travelling through Spain. We didn't need to dig two layers of rooms for gravity flow to do the same job. A hillside is too limiting especially for expansion, but we have no slope anyway.'

Peter focuses on the vineyard, even helping regularly with pruning, bunch thinning and leaf plucking. That's where most of the quality-versus-quantity issues are resolved, he reckons.

Peter Caldwell: 'The vintage itself is very short, whereas we have a whole year to plan for it. We treat everything as if it's all going into the Reserve. Otherwise you're selling yourself short. Ninety per cent of the effort has gone in by time we've picked.

'With hand-picking, it's difficult to get a reasonable amount of fruit through in a short time. The machine harvester allows us to pick fruit when we think it's at its optimum level. Some companies pick some [fruit] before it's ready, then as much as they can at the right time, then maybe another twenty per cent after it's too far, because that's just the best way they can do it. With a machine, we try and maximise the chances of picking everything at the right time.

'Of course machine harvesting means we don't have the fruit selection in the vineyard that you get with hand-picking. So we built the conveyor [inspection] belt to allow a couple of people to take out things we would have left in the vineyard if we were working by hand.'

Te Kairanga is still expanding, both on the Martinborough Terrace and farther afield. After intensive soil and climate research, sites at Ruakokoputuna and Spring Rock were identified and developed. A no-compromise approach featuring top grafted clonal selections and high density planting has paid off, and the Chardonnay and Pinot Noir have shown excellent growth in their first two years. However Peter reckons it will be ten years before they are truly proven. Watch this space.

Palliser Estate

Pam Ryan

Driving into Martinborough from Wellington or Greytown, it's the first winery you pass – and the biggest. Palliser is the heavyweight around here, with an annual crush of over 600 tonnes – but that's small to medium by national standards: indicating the boutique nature of much of the local industry.

Palliser Estate metamorphosed in 1987 from the Om Santi partnership set up in 1983. Wyatt Creech instigated both. Wyatt has worn many hats in his long and energetic working life: farmer, businessman, accountant and government minister. His matter-of-fact recall of the establishment of two of the most successful local vineyards, is like delving into a well-oiled database.

During the seven years prior to Palliser's birth, the infant Martinborough industry had been learning to walk. But at the time, not everyone thought it a prudent endeavour.

Wyatt Creech: 'It was maybe '84 when some MAF [Ministry of Agriculture and Fisheries] people from Hastings came down and offered to organise a seminar. They put up screens showing consumption was falling and production was racing up. When these two trends intersected there would be a surplus. It was pretty gloomy stuff. The MAF guy seriously doubted the wisdom of planting vinafera varieties. The only commercial variety in New Zealand he recommended was Müller Thurgau.

'We never had any more to do with MAF. They were in the wrong head space. In retrospect I thought they were very busybody to come down and suggest we should come and listen to them. We were risking our capital. They weren't risking a bean.

'The moment farming became out of the ordinary, and people were putting up their own capital, especially in deer and goats etcetera, MAF advice was dodgy, because they were just driven by the conventions.

'Despite that negative MAF advice we've done well, but it's taken twenty years.'

Vines had been planted in 1985, under the Om Santi incarnation, but the first Palliser wine was made in 1989 by Larry McKenna at Martinborough Vineyard. It won gold. Allan Johnson was appointed winemaker at the end of 1990. While working in Western Australia, he'd noted Martinborough's emergence.

Allan Johnson: 'My mother used to send me newspapers, so I knew that Martinborough was showing promise. A lot of this followed the success of Larry McKenna. The area had obviously proven itself with the wines of Martinborough Vineyards, Ata Rangi and Dry River. A strong reputation was already established.

'Palliser was second generation. The others were ten years ahead, so naturally it took a while before Palliser wines were talked about in the same vein.'

The earliest vineyard had been exclusively Pinot Noir and Chardonnay, but as Palliser established, Sauvignon Blanc was planted to balance the

Palliser Wine

Palliser is the among the best examples of Martinborough's varietal scope. The Palliser Chardonnay, Riesling, Sauvignon Blanc and Pinot Noir all regularly attain five star ratings from wine commentators. They also produce a lush and concentrated Noble Chardonnay, a finely balanced Pinot Gris and an attractive yeasty Méthode Champenoise.

Palliser's second tier brand, Pencarrow, has been described as different in style rather than in quality. Both the Pinot Noir and Sauvignon offer quality and value often not matched by first tier labels.

range. The industry is prone to fashion changes, and this strategy gave Allan wider scope, with more varieties to work with. He won gold with his first two wines: the 1991 Riesling (grown on contract) and 1991 Sauvignon Blanc.

Allan Johnson: 'We aim very much for wines that are clearly their varieties, with good intensity of fruit flavour, richness and roundness and harmony. We're looking for a balance and an absence of bitter phenolics. We're trying to put pleasure into a bottle.'

Growth offers Allan the opportunity to introduce technology that reduces effort, yet increases his control.

Allan Johnson: 'Though we've expanded facilities, it's still a batch operation. We have equipment to make the wine-making easier. So we can still pay the attention required to each separate batch without having to sweat and labour over it. We can put the intellectual energy in.

Machine harvesting for instance, offers advantages over hand-picking. We can get in early in the morning and pick grapes when they're cold. That's good for Pinot Noir, which is typically put through cold maceration.

In any of the trials I've seen between machine harvested and hand-picked fruit, people have not been able to spot the difference in the wine. You'd think that the fruit coming in from hand-picking should be better: whole bunches, no pedicels, [stalks] etcetera. But we pay special attention to our mechanical harvesting. We always go through the vineyard beforehand and take off any second set [bunches] or whatever, so we are only harvesting what we want. We have a very good machine and a good de-stemmer/crusher that separates out any leaf material or pedicels. Our wine may be influenced [by machine harvesting] but we can't taste it.'

When not looking after Palliser's grapes, Allan tends six acres of his own Pinot Noir at the beginning of the Ruakokoputuna Terrace.

In 1988, Wyatt Creech entered Parliament. Promoted to minister in 1990, he was no longer able to work in the business. So Richard Riddiford took the wheel at almost the same time as Allan came on board. As Allan

Richard Riddiford, Palliser Estate.
Pam Ryan

revved up production, Richard cranked the marketing.

If Stan Chifney was the grandfather of Martinborough wine, Richard Riddiford is the godfather. His Mephistophelian smile only partly masks a blunt authority. But Richard acknowledges he started from scratch.

Richard Riddiford: 'When I made an investment in Palliser, I never dreamed for a moment that sitting here twenty years later, we'd export to eighteen countries and in effect have the beginnings of a global brand.

'When Wyatt Creech put together the original partnership, we didn't really know what we were doing, to be honest. There were no models. We suddenly discovered that we could make great wine and that we could export it to the world.

'The fascinating thing about the New Zealand wine industry is that there are very passionate, driven people involved. People have been prepared to travel globally and sell the product. And it wasn't done by people with MBAs from Harvard or anything. It's been done by people who are very proud of what they have produced, and they've travelled the world selling it.'

Previous work in meat and game exports made Richard acutely aware of product differentiation, so his over-riding goal is placing the Palliser brand at the top end of the market.

Richard Riddiford: 'Whatever you're trying to sell, if you don't have a great product that is also well branded, you end up in a commodity sector, which is not the place to be.'

His second preoccupation is the Martinborough brand.

Richard Riddiford: 'Vast areas of the world still haven't heard of New Zealand wine, so when we travel, that's the most important brand we represent. The second most important brand is Martinborough.

'Martinborough has runs on the board and has hit a few centuries. It has the longest history of producing world-class Pinot in the country.

'It also has four or five vineyards producing quite different Pinots, but in addition to that specialty, one of the great strengths of the district is the range of wines. It's very good.'

Palliser has focussed on attaining high objective standards. In 1995 it was the first winery in New Zealand to achieve ISO 9002 certification. But meeting those standards is pointless if they can't be sustained. That realisation led Palliser to adopt strict environmental standards too, and, in league with Martinborough Vineyard, Vidals and C. J. Pask, to develop an environmental management system. In 1998, the four vineyards became the first in the world to be certified ISO 14001.

Richard Riddiford: 'Environment is now our number one priority. If we alter either the soils or the climate, through what we put into either the atmosphere or the soil, then we don't have a business. We were recent converts; it suddenly struck us one day that our environment was absolutely key to our survival.'

Systems up and running smoothly, Richard Riddiford is back in his office calling the purchasing manager of a prestigious Singapore hotel. They offer the worlds best wines, according to their advertisement. 'Not possible.' says Riddiford. 'You don't have ours.'

They do now.

The Bordeaux Brigade

Among the earliest vines planted in Martinborough was the traditional Bordeaux variety, Cabernet Sauvignon. Bordeaux red, called Claret in Britain, is usually a combination of Cabernet Sauvignon, Merlot and Cabernet Franc. Burgundian red, in contrast, is straight Pinot Noir.

Ata Rangi, Martinborough Vineyard and Chifney Wines all planted Cabernet Sauvignon. Stan Chifney vindicated that choice in 1985, when his first competition offering went gold. Pinot Noir, hardly a popular variety at the time, was also planted, and quickly produced wine quite unlike previous, local, lightweight Pinots. Larry McKenna's stunning successes for Martinborough Vineyard from 1986 on, and Ata Rangi's international trophies, established the town as the country's Pinot Noir capital. Derek Milne's early comparisons to the Côte d'Or were borne out. Pinot Noir dominated new planting from the early 1990s, and is now clearly the flagship of the Wairarapa's armada of wine offerings. Regional marketing spotlights the variety, and touts the area as the Antipodean Burgundy.

This predominance isn't simply a matter of prizes. Pinot Noir can be ripened comfortably in Martinborough nine years out of ten. Even in the tenth year it's pretty good. Cabernet might manage five or six. Unfortunately, Cabernet Sauvignon made from unripe fruit often displays an excessively herbaceous character, rather like green leaves. Such wine isn't flattered by comparison with the full, ripe examples Australia produces cheaply and reliably year after year.

But despite Pinot's ascendancy, a determined band of Bordeaux-philes labours on, defying majority opinion and marketing clout, and producing some fine Bordeaux-style red, despite the odds.

The Turakirae Reserve Cabernet Sauvignon/Franc and the Petra Cab Sav are Winslow's big hitters. In good vintages their Rosetta Cabernet Rose is also a class act.

Winslow

Steve Tarring used to be a research technician; one of several Martinborough winemakers with a strong scientific background.

His previous work took him overseas, but he and his wife Jennifer bought land before they went, and had it planted under contract. Every year they came home for at least pruning, before eventually returning permanently. With his experience and confidence developed over more than a decade of vintages, Steve can now pursue an ambition to create his favourite Bordeaux style red. To that end he has taken over the wine-making from Strat Canning, who worked for Winslow part-time for several years.

Steve Tarring: 'I like Bordeaux varieties, and I had an image in my taste memory of what I would like to produce as a wine. We wanted to make a Grave style blend, which is predominantly Cab Sav, with twenty per cent Cab Franc and ten per cent Merlot. So accordingly we planted the vineyard; naively, I have to admit now. The plants didn't subscribe to my master plan. We ended up with Merlot that didn't really flower properly, and Franc that wouldn't produce it's twenty per cent quota. Nonetheless, we were making a Bordeaux style which was really running against the grain of what other people here were doing.'

Winslow's Turakirae Reserve Cabernet Sauvignon/Franc justified Steve's faith, winning gold in both Britain and New Zealand. Winslow's Petra Cabernet Sauvignon also commands a respectful following.

Steve Tarring: 'My chief motivation was that I wanted to craft a wine true to my standards and that allowed me to be honest in the evaluation of the finished product. Over the last twelve vintages we've been moving slowly but surely to that point. Now I'm happier than I've ever been with the style of wine we are producing.

What I think we should do as a region is drop this pretence that we are part of France, and stop making all these analogies between what happens in Burgundy and what happens in Martinborough. For instance, there are no olive trees in Burgundy. Here we have commercial plantations of them. So isn't this more like Tuscany? Focussing on Pinot Noir tends to bias the focus of some wine writers. In the end we do our own thing and polish our craft.'

Pam Ryan

'Comparing our styles with French wine is a shame too, because they are a different style and that's their strength. For example, our 2001 Pinot Noir is more Burgundian, and we were accused of being too European. When overseas buyers open our bottle, they expect a New Zealand taste and character rather than a copy.' Mike Finucane

Claddagh

Suzann Pearless: 'The first day I came to Martinborough, in February 1992, I met a winemaker, and my first experience of the place was an argument about the respective merits of growing Pinot or Cabernet here. That argument continues.'

Suzann and husband Russell Pearless didn't come to Martinborough looking for controversy or even a lifestyle. They alighted in Martinborough on the wings of serendipity.

Suzann Pearless: 'I'm an Aussie. I was working in New York, and got a short project in Wellington where I met Russell. We were both in the computer business. We were invited to Martinborough for the Craft Fair. I was pregnant, having believed I couldn't get pregnant, and I couldn't sleep. I had no intention of living in New Zealand, but I got up in the morning and said to Russell, "This is where I want to live and bring up our child." It was a complete epiphany. We arrived on Saturday and bought land on the Sunday.'

Richard Pearless, Claddagh.

Pam Ryan

The Pearless's varietal choices were somewhat unorthodox too. Claddagh planted both Bordeaux and Burgundy.

Suzann Pearless: 'We approach production in a different way. We have no shareholders or partners, so we make the wines we like. Fortunately we like a range of wines, because that spreads the risk. But every wine has to be great.

'We ripen Cab Sav every year. We don't irrigate and we crop really low. We are absolutely brutal in the way we manage our vines. Russell is the winemaker who will blink last. He will drop half an already low crop without hesitation. We ripen the amount of Cabernet Sauvignon it is possible to ripen in any year.

'All our Pinot Noir is Abel or 10-5. We won't go into Dijon clones.

'Martinborough Pinot Noir is characterised by layers of flavour. That's what you get from Abel. We planted it in the roughest part of our vineyard. In the '98 drought we lost a third of our six-year-old vines, and we didn't make commercial Pinot Noir until the vines were ten years old. So we get beautiful rich flavours.

'Irrigated versus non-irrigated has been a big argument for a long time. Neil McCallum was a key influence in our going non-irrigated. You can taste the concentration in the wine. The cost is enormous and the penalties are high. It takes forever to get the first crop, and even then the yield is low.'

Russell and Suzann don't see Claddagh ever crushing a vintage of more than 25 tonnes. But then they don't see wine as all they have to offer. Suzann is a foodie. Verjus and varietal wine jellies are produced, and public and private barbeques, picnics and food festivals are organised in the vineyard. If the food incubates as well as their wine, Claddagh is on track as an epicure's larder.

'It was a complete epiphany. We arrived on Saturday and bought land on the Sunday.'
Suzann Pearless

Claddagh Wines
For many years Claddagh sold its fruit to other wineries. When finally released under their own label, all their wines hit the ground running. Claddagh Pinot Noir, Merlot and Cab Sav have all been mentioned enthusiastically in dispatches and competitions, and their 2002 Sauvignon Blanc gained a silver medal.

A label to watch.

Benfield & Delamare

Bill Benfield: 'We are the same latitude as Portugal and slightly hotter
than Bordeaux.'

Bill Benfield and Sue Delamare have been described as the Bordeaux
Brigade's most vociferous partisans. They prefer 'vigorous advocates'.
Whichever, there's no doubting their passion for Cabernet Sauvignon and
Merlot-based reds, and their genuine belief that the Martinborough wine
'establishment' has consistently disparaged winemakers and wines that don't
conform to the marketing mantra of a few key Pinot Noir producers.

Bill's family connections with the liquor trade exposed him to wine
from a very early age, unusual at the time, he reckons. As an architect in
the 1970s, Bill worked in Wellington with David Bloomfield. From David
he imbibed Masterton's early winemaking history, and watched Bloomfield's vineyard evolve. Bill and Sue visited the Wairarapa several times
looking for land, until they spied a For Sale sign tacked on an old barn in
Martinborough. A deal was struck and they bought the plot. Two more
pieces of land were subsequently purchased and planted, giving Benfield
and Delamare a little over 2.5 hectares in total. Of that, just over half is
planted in Merlot, forty per cent in Cabernet Sauvignon and the rest, in
Cabernet Franc.

Bill Benfield: 'We looked at all the information available such as weather
and soil stats, and of course Chifneys' '86 Cab Sav had taken gold at
the Air New Zealand awards. So we decided to go with Bordeaux reds.
'We went for close planting on a low trellis, which we dropped by
another 200 millimetres about three or four years after the initial planting. We went to France around '89 and saw vineyards around Pomerol
with fruit wires at 400 millimetres off the ground, while ours were 600
millimetres. We tried that and found it gave us an advantage so we
changed the whole vineyard.'

That regime of low trellis to absorb ground heat, close planting and
extremely light cropping, soon produced results. Benfield and Delamare's
1991 offering took gold at the Air New Zealand awards, and was included
in 1993, in *Cuisine's* ten best New Zealand reds. Their 1990 Bordeaux style

Bill and Sue's premium wine is Benfield and Delamare Martinborough. The second string to their Bordeaux bow is the early drinking Song for Osiris.

Bill Benfield and Sue Delamare.
Pam Ryan

red won a gold medal at the Intervin Competition in Canada. Bill doesn't mince words on how he sees the comparison between Burgundy and Bordeaux in the district.

Bill Benfield: 'In terms of awards, the tiny Cabernet Sauvignon production here is more medal-encrusted per litre produced than the enormous wash of Pinot Noir. We don't enter local competitions now. They are just looking for regional expression. We sell out each year, but it would be good to be selling for a higher price.'

Benfield and Delamare sell their tiny annual production of around 300 cases mainly by mail order, some to the United States; and some to a few specialist wine shops.

Harvest hardware. *Pam Ryan*

'We are lifestylers, but it isn't romantic. It's hard graft. The learning curve was steep, but interesting.' Roz Walker

Alexander Vineyard

Mike Finucane: 'Although it's on the edge for it, people make good Cab Sav here. The 1998 Te Kairanga Cab Sav was grown close by. But the marketing message around here is Pinot Noir. We wanted a foot clearly in both [Burgundian and Bordeaux] camps.'

Alexander owners Mike Finucane and partner Roz Walker are relatively late on the Martinborough scene. Arriving from England in 1996, they were immediately struck by the varieties the area could produce, and produce well.

Mike Finucane: 'It's really quite remarkable. Such great wines of so many different varieties. All from within the square mile, as I describe Martinborough itself. That's not climatic differences. There's great Riesling and good Syrah here, within spitting distance of great Pinot Noir and of course Chardonnay. We have good Cab Franc and great Cab/Merlot coming out for 2001. We feel it's better than 1998 which was supposed to be the vintage of the century for Cabernet wines in New Zealand.

'There's a regionalisation of New Zealand going on. Hawkes Bay is Bordeaux, Otago is Pinot Noir, Marlborough was Sauvignon Blanc but now with Pinot Noir coming through. Martinborough is Pinot country. It's a bit of "four legs good, two legs bad. A bit of a shame".'

Mike also has reservations about assuming that good New Zealand wine must stylistically mimic its Old World counterparts.

'Comparing our styles with French wine is a shame too, because they are a different style and that's their strength. For example, our 2001 Pinot Noir is more Burgundian, and we were accused of being too European. When overseas buyers open our bottle, they expect a New Zealand taste and character rather than a copy.'

Rather than choosing to grow and make just one red or the other, a foot in each camp was Mike and Roz's original intention. But a business partnership break-up prompted a repositioning and rationalising of vineyard sites.

Alexander Wines

Until a couple of years back, Alexander's star was their Reserve Cabernet/Merlot. However with consolidation on their home vineyard, the focus will switch to Pinot Noir which will grow in stature as the vines age. Also look out for stand-alone Merlot and Cabernet Franc.

Pinot Noir will make up over ninety per cent of Alexander's planting in the future. The rest will be Merlot and Cabernet Franc.

In his previous life, Mike was a chartered surveyor. Ros is a clinical psychologist. Transplanting their family to another hemisphere, and plunging into a business they had no background in, was gutsy but scary stuff.

Roz Walker: 'My Mum lives here. We were over here on a trip. Thinking about going back home to England I thought, "Oh God, twenty-five more years ahead of me. What do we do?" I remember Mike saying "Well, I like fishing and I like wine, but I can't imagine making a living out of fishing". Then for some reason it just started to snowball.

'When we got here neither of us had a job, and we knew nothing about wine-making or vineyard management or establishment; with by that time two children. It seemed like madness, really. I still work as a psychologist part of the week. Mike was going to get a job, but after six weeks it became clear the property business was in the past. Been there done that. We are lifestylers, but it isn't romantic. It's hard graft. The learning curve was steep, but interesting.'

Mike Finucane: 'When our erstwhile [vineyard] partners moved on just before vintage, we hired a consultant winemaker, Elise Montgomery, and we still use her. A very talented winemaker. Elise shouts at me through emails, sends me the magic recipe, comes over and checks the wine. We are maybe advanced cellarhands now.

'As the vines get older, so do we. I didn't know which end of a hoe to use in 1996. Now we are amazed by the difference between two different barrels from the same manufacturer, say one from Nievre, and the other from Allier. We had none of that knowledge at the start.

'Part of my old job was marketing, and with contacts back in the UK that has helped. We've exported to Britain, Malaysia and Japan.

'We are aiming to send the bulk of production overseas, but have to build up our local market as well. However, the supermarkets will want mainly large producers.

'I'm very cynical about wine competitions, but I'd love to win one, because that's what guides the consumer. People just want the reassurance of a medal, even when the previous year's vintage was as good.'

Michael Mebus – Mebus Estate: 'It's pure arrogance for people to call their area either Burgundy or Bordeaux. It took the French five hundred bloody years to determine what should grow where. A Kiwi can not tell me after twenty years that this or that is the Holy Grail. The argument is borderline stupidity.'

Strat Canning – Margrain and Stratford: 'Some people have bet their lives on Cabernet. But the stats don't support that. I used to make Winslows' wines from '94 to '99. We made some really good wines. And we make perfectly good Cabernet types at Margrain too. But we couldn't sell as much Cabernet as we do Pinot Noir. That's the reality. It's not a large-scale commercial proposition. But good luck to them. We need to give people a choice in Martinborough.'

Bordeaux-style reds will always be in the minority around Martinborough, and the Wairarapa as a whole. But they will undoubtedly continue to be grown, with exceptional examples produced in warm seasons like 1998.

However, just as Bordeaux producers blend differing proportions of Cabernet Sauvignon, Merlot and Cabernet Franc, depending on the vintage and its weather, so too are Wairarapa winemakers evolving their own 'best combinations', which in some cases bear only nominal resemblance to the wines that inspired them. Indeed, that's the case with both Pinot Noir and Cab Sav blends. Increasingly, growers and winemakers are exploring how best to achieve a top quality local expression, rather than slavishly mimicking an overseas style.

Ata Rangi's Célèbre is a good illustration of that trend. It's almost a map of how Ata Rangi dealt with the tension between Bordeaux and Burgundy. The 1986 Célèbre was seventy per cent Cabernet Sauvignon. The 2000 version was Syrah/Merlot dominant, with only forty per cent Cab Sav, as if Clive and Ollie have found an equilibrium somewhere between Bordeaux and the Southern Rhône. In fact, their blend is pure Martinborough.

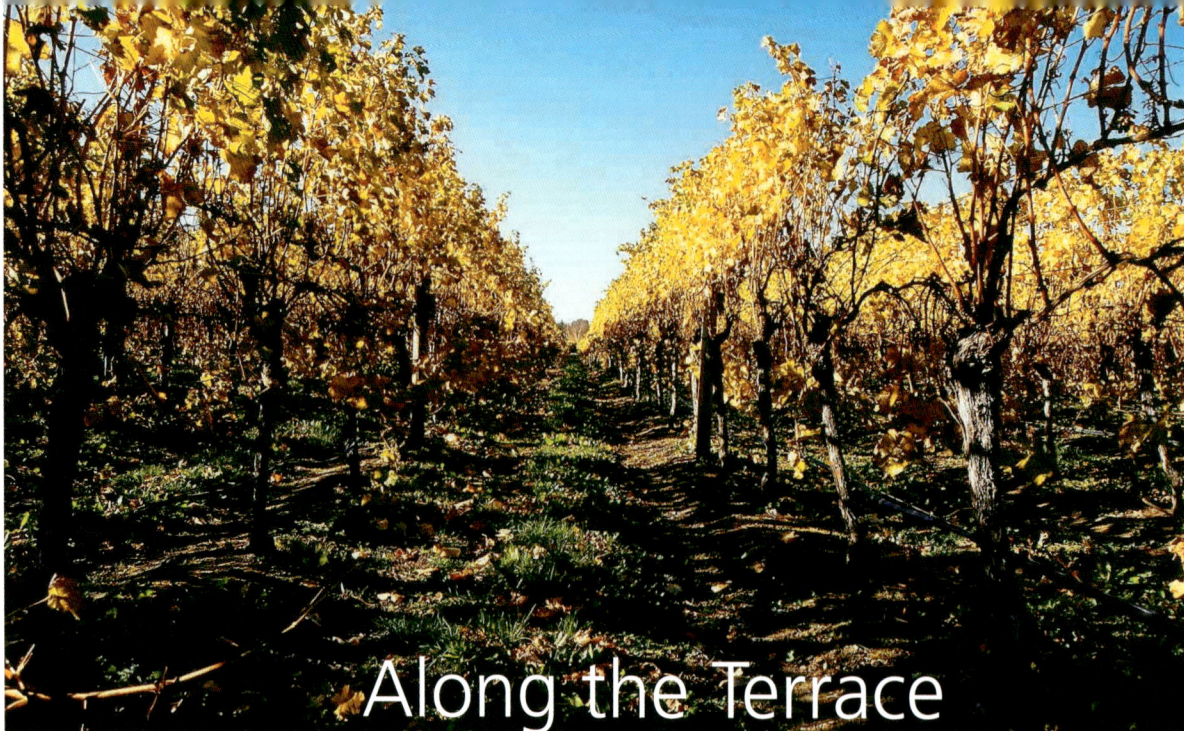

Along the Terrace

Pam Ryan

The first vineyards planted in Martinborough were scattered along an old river terrace above the Huangarua and Ruamahanga Rivers. The outer line or escarpment of that terrace is most plainly seen when driving into town from Wellington. Palliser Estate perches on the very edge of it.

Imagine a line drawn diagonally north-west to south-east through the Martinborough town square. The area between that line and the escarpment edge to the north is broadly known as the Martinborough Terrace. Virtually every vineyard in town sits on that. In fact, the Martinborough Terrace Appellation actually applies to an even more restricted area. The Martinborough Terrace Appellation was set up in 1986; the founding members of the organising committee being Chifney Wines, Ata Rangi, Dry River and Martinborough Vineyard. Soil types, a maximum rainfall of 800 millimetres and wine style parameters were the criteria used to identify the appellation area. The resulting south-western border of the zone is a line drawn between a couple of specific trig points. Producers within the precinct who meet all the requirements can carry the appellation seal on their bottles. Eight producers eventually qualified.

The appellation caused, and still causes, considerable friction in the local wine community. Its proponents set it up as a way to define and protect the reputation of a specific and special growing area with a proven track record. The appellation's opponents on the other hand, some of whom are literally a stone's throw over the line, claim it's simply an arbitrary marketing device designed to give vineyards within the hallowed area an exclusive advantage. Moreover, vineyards subsequently planted a few kilometres out of town, on the Te Muna Terrace, argue that any appellation should be based solely on soil and climate parameters. Under those more objective criteria, they claim, their plantings would qualify as much as any other. The quarrel became further complicated when some appellation supporters bought grapes from outside Martinborough. They can't use the seal on wine made from that fruit, of course, but the issue was hardly clarified in the minds of the buying public as a consequence.

Richard Riddiford – Palliser Estate: 'If you're saying that in Martinborough we have five different appellations, you are going down the French route, which is very complex, and will confuse the market.'

Steve Smith – Craggy Range: 'Appellation should be determined by soil and climate, not style or typicality. You can't line up ten Pinot Noirs made on the Martinborough Terrace and say they are all the same. It makes it incredibly political and divisive. And if it's just geographical, different soils within the same area could both be called Martinborough Terrace. That can't be right. I think what defines Martinborough Terrace needs to be soil type, and anyone with that soil type can be in.'

Larry McKenna – The Escarpment Vineyard: 'The appellation is like reinventing a class system. They want to create something like Romeny Conti or Romanée-St-Vivant.

'My view is that it's about two hundred years too early. It's a long time before the market will think about wines in that detail in this country. Overseas I find it difficult to get the word New Zealand across let alone Martinborough. If you get the message Martinborough Pinot Noir across you've done fantastically. If you get your brand across, you're a bloody genius.'

Gary Voss – Voss Estate: 'My point of view is that Te Muna Terrace is just the next bend round the river, and that someone in London probably doesn't care about the difference. It illustrates the danger of thinking the world stops at the end of your drive.

'They looked into appellations here in the eighties and I think they decided it was easier to negotiate peace in the Middle East.'

John Comerford – wine judge: 'When the classification appellation issue arose, the question was whether there should be a quality perspective introduced. I encouraged them not to have quality parameters – because essentially they'd be adjudicating on their own – but to assist each other and promote the region. The Champagne region is the best example of that. The consumer ultimately decides whether the quality is there.'

Neil McCallum – Dry River: 'When the appellation was set up, its purpose was to protect the public's understanding of what Martinborough Terrace means and the type of wine you would expect from it.

'Martinborough Terrace is a legally defined name applying legally defined boundaries based around soil type and less than a specified rainfall. The definition allows other areas to use the name Martinborough Terrace by two routes. Either by showing that the soil is the same and the rainfall less than 800 millimetres; or by showing that the wines produced are similar in type. The former is much more objective, and therefore the preferred way to show compliance.

'We need to protect the brand, just as we needed to create it.'

———

There are over two dozen vineyards, some minuscule, scattered across the greater Martinborough Terrace. Observing the appellation dispute from the safety of the outside, it's ironic that regardless of appellation qualification wines from Martinborough, and increasingly from the wider Wairarapa area, are of consistently high quality: across a range of vineyards, across a number of vintages, and across several varieties. No other New Zealand wine-producing area can lay claim to anything like that depth and degree of consistency.

———

Pam Ryan

Of the two Pinots, Porter's Pinot Noir sets the pace. The Gris will appeal if you prefer a big ripe style.

Porter's Pinot

John Porter: 'In 1989, after two big cases, I really needed a break from the law. We went over to Burgundy and Tuscany and walked through the vineyards and tasted a lot. It was charming. Came back and in Baxters restaurant in Wellington I drank a glass of Larry McKenna's Sauvignon Blanc. Then an '89 Dry River Riesling. I was stunned. I'd just come back from a month around the grape heartland of the world. I thought, "I've gone 12,000 miles to do this, and I come back and here it is, right on my doorstep".

'That weekend I came to Martinborough and had a look around. Within three months we'd bought an old house with an acre and planted the grapes.'

John Porter has the stature of a front row prop, the voice of an operatic baritone, and the enthusiasm of a Boxer puppy. Enthusiasm was pretty much all he and his wife Annabel Clayton had going for them at the beginning.

John Porter: 'I didn't know what I was doing. A great deal of soul searching went on about how tall to make the posts, how far apart to plant the vines, how wide to make the rows. I got lots of conflicting advice. You never knew who to believe.

'I ordered exactly 624 plants. It was grafted stock. They were left on the back step, and I had to get someone round to reassure me that I'd been sent the right thing.

'But I decided Pinot Noir was the grape. I just think it's the most romantic, the most wonderful… Burgundy is the wine for me.

'We put them in the ground and they grew! We got a crop in '95. I did everything by hand: no tractor. It was fantastic. I was sneaking days off work. I'd drive over, work my guts out all day and then drive home [to Wellington] and do a case next day. I just loved it.

'When the five acres came up we bought that. That turned out to be a financial pit. I took cuttings that I liked from around the neighbourhood.

'There was a hierarchy here. First the locals who had been here over a hundred years. Then the first tier of grape-growers. They were a bit wary. They didn't really encourage people with open arms. Obviously they were protecting their interests. I admire people like Neil [McCallum]. He brought me here. Well, *he* didn't, but his wine did. And Clive [Paton]. They came here with virtually no money and put their balls on the line. I was very aware that this was their livelihood and I tread very carefully. But I was desperate for knowledge and they were helpful.

'The second wave of guys like Strat [Canning] and Roger [Parkinson] came with the classical wine education. They were my peers in age terms and I got on well with them and learned a lot.

'It's a fantastic place to live: a great place to bring up kids. And to have turned a stony paddock into a vineyard that produces Pinot Noir of international quality, gives us a great sense of satisfaction.'

John and Annabel moved to Martinborough in 1998, and now have just on two hectares planted: ninety per cent in Pinot Noir, ten per cent in Pinot Gris, and a hundred olive trees. As they both still work as lawyers, it's hardly a laid-back lifestyle.

John Porter: 'I say to Annie, "We're living a dream". But when you're putting the nets on at midday at 30 degrees and the kids are screaming, there's precious little romance. We have no permanent staff, and don't want to buy a lot of gear. So it's a bit of a peasant existence. We just get finished vintage and we have to pick the olives.'

The pair obviously do something right. Their 600 case annual production is soon sold out. Porter's Pinot has slotted very respectably into the quality end of the Martinborough market. That, John says, is no reason to rest on their laurels.

John Porter: 'The wines that are coming out now are not just better, they are totally different creatures. The bar has got higher. People are expecting more. They are more knowledgable. New Zealand might just redefine the boundaries of certain wines.'

Roger Parkinson, Nga Waka.
Pam Ryan

Nga Waka Vineyard

When Roger Parkinson set up Nga Waka, he aimed to produce only white wines: classy, bone-dry, crafted-to-cellar white wines. And he did. In fact, his first vintage 1993 Sauvignon Blanc won gold. He wasn't convinced back in 1988, that Martinborough Pinot Noir, despite its early success, was going to be an international hit.

Roger Parkinson: 'Funnily enough, more of my experience in Australia and in France was with red wine. But I knew early on that we had something special with our white wines that would give us a place overseas. The competition with red wine is tougher and our climate generally is more marginal for red wine. There was a lot of hype about Pinot in New Zealand early on, but Bordeaux-style wines in New Zealand, for instance, had always been a bit lean and green.

'All the other winemakers laughed and said "You'll be growing Pinot Noir one day", and sure enough we soon were. But it was the mid-nineties before I thought we had enough information to be confident about moving in that direction.

'Our initial success with white wine made it more comfortable financially to get into Pinot Noir.'

A teacher by training, and a trainer by profession, Roger subsequently gained a viticultural and wine-making qualification from Roseworthy College in Australia. But what spurred him into the wine industry initially?

Roger Parkinson: 'Dad worked for Foreign Affairs for forty years. So half my childhood was spent overseas. My parents were posted in Paris and got hooked on wine and we kids got to have the dregs at the bottom of the bottles. That was really where the interest in wine came from.

'I regard around 1980 as the start of the modern New Zealand wine industry. The shift was just starting to happen from the old, fortified, hybrid-dominated industry, to the modern industry, and some really smart wines were just starting to show. We got interested. Lots of tastings and going up to Hawkes Bay and coming back with too much wine that we really couldn't afford.

'Then from the early eighties the first Martinborough wines to make a real impression came through. I was working in Wellington then, so it was close to home.

'The thing that interested me was that the plantings here had developed as a result of good research rather than – as is often the case – around cultural or population hubs. Martinborough was the first place (along with Marlborough to some extent) where there was an attempt to identify what grape varieties would work.

'From 1985 we started looking for land.

'I did a correspondence course to get my chemistry sorted out. I knew I needed that, because I knew I was going to go and get a qualification somewhere and do it properly. It's even harder now. I don't think you would even consider getting into grape-growing and wine-making now without up-to-date tertiary qualifications and experience. The days of the enthusiastic amateur are history, with maybe the odd exception.'

There's nothing amateur about the Nga Waka set-up. The vineyard gateways and drive are edged in crisp, rectangular wire baskets of river stones. The contemporary concrete and corrugated steel winery verges on industrial chic. Its ordered, uncluttered interior exudes an air of focussed passion: no-nonsense and unembellished, but anything but prosaic.

Roger Parkinson: 'There's no future in Martinborough for cheap wine. We are all smaller or small-scale wineries. We all do more hands-on work than you could for ten dollars per bottle.

'We really work to get quality. What you do in the winery is important and you have to get things right there, but you are not really adding quality to the wine as you can in the vineyard.

Nga Waka Wines

'Immaculate', 'delicate', 'classy' and 'finesse' are the adjectives applied to Nga Waka wines. Riesling, Chardonnay, Sauvignon Blanc and Pinot Noir: all are full-flavoured, well integrated and designed to cellar.

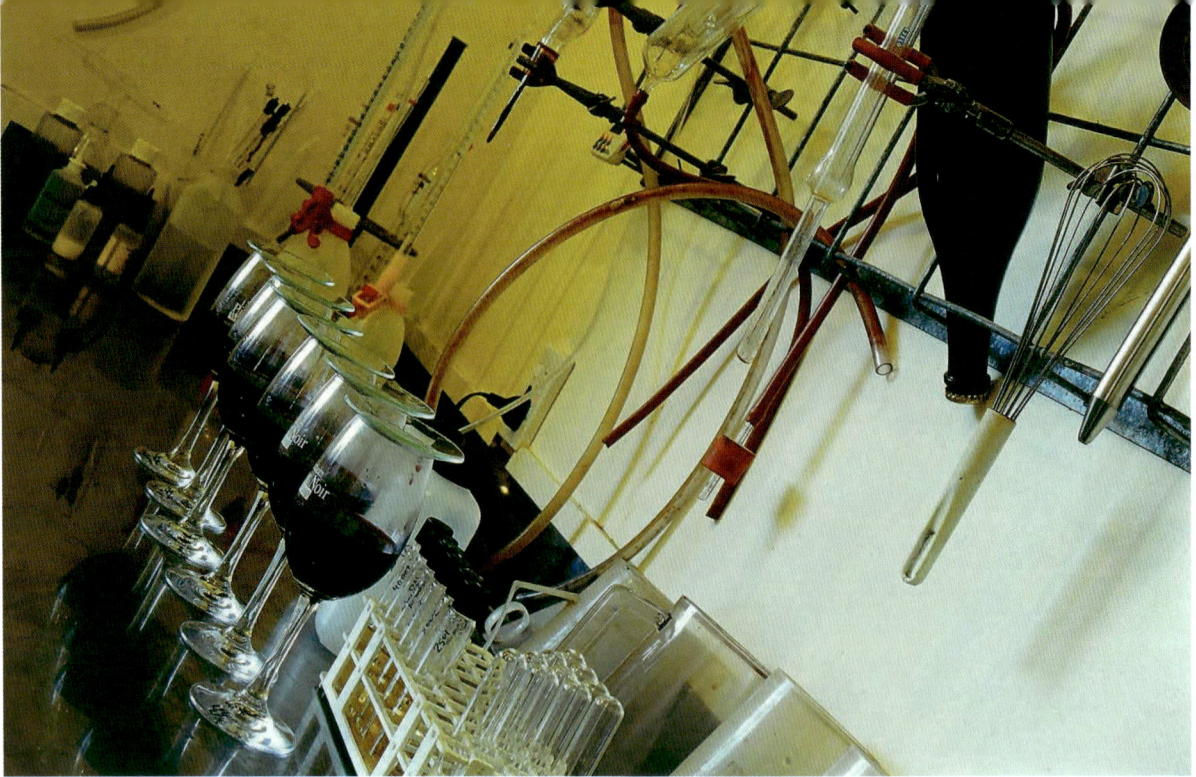

Wine options. *Pam Ryan*

'Because of the way we choose to handle it, Sauvignon Blanc is the most labour intensive for us. It's a fantastic variety. Other people say it grows like a weed and you just snip it off. But if you do the work you can justify the price. You can't reproduce that attention to detail on a grand scale. Riesling is the easiest variety to work with. Chardonnay and Pinot Noir take a bit more effort.

'From older vines we should be starting to see more structure, complexity, depth and maturity. It's partly a function of vine age, but also of greater grape-grower and winemaker experience.

'For me, what characterises Martinborough wines is something about length and strength through the palate. Especially with Riesling, we have a combination of elegance and strength. We maintain it with low cropping levels.

'The enthusiasm for Pinot Gris is largely domestic. I don't think we'll make a hit overseas with it – but I'm happy to be proven wrong.

'I still aim for bone-dry wines. We want to make fine Martinborough wine, and the first thing that predicates fine wine is its ability to improve with age. My belief is that dry wines always express better with age, than wines that might have early charm because of residual sugar.

'When people ask "What's your favourite from the wines you produce?" I can't answer that. It's like asking, which is your favourite kid?'

Muirlea Rise

Willie Brown was a full-blooded Rabelaisian character; bursting with forthright opinions, quirky asides and exuberant salesmanship to the very end of his life. In the retail, and then the wholesale, wine industry most of his working career, Willie earned a formidable reputation for his reliable and astute wine advice. As he approached fifty, Willie's wife Lea – not a retiring person in her own right – tried to persuade him to buy a bach.

Lea Brown: 'He wasn't a golfer or a club member, but I couldn't see the point of working the same way until you drop dead. It didn't make sense to me. But Willie was a bit obdurate, like a lot of men. I asked him one day, "What do you want to be doing in ten years time?" Willie said "I'll always like wine." So I said "Why don't you get a little land and have a vineyard, and make the wine you want to make?"'

Willie Brown: 'But where? At first I thought around Auckland because that's where we were living. But no. I wanted to go to Martinborough because I love Pinot and there were some very interesting Pinots coming out of there.'

So when the Browns set up in Martinborough in 1987, Willie had to plant Pinot Noir, and it had to be Malcolm Abel's clone, which was brought to prominence at Ata Rangi. Willie had tasted Abel's Pinot Noir years before. At the time he was 'back room boy' preparing samples for the Tourist Hotel Corporation wine competition, a job he did for nine years. Impressed by what Malcolm had produced, Willie asked the chief judge to sample the young Pinot. 'Great potential!' was the verdict and Willie's judgement was vindicated. He remembered the clone.

Willie Brown: 'Pinot Noir is a wine you either like or dislike. It's a layer thing. Ever since I was introduced to wine at Granny's birthday, when I was given a glass of Asti diluted with lemonade, I got bitten by the bug. How on earth could you get so many different flavours out of a single grape?'

'My Pinot Noir is an old-fashioned, "fine wine" style. That's what intrigues me. Fine Pinots have such elegance and finesse about them. They're feminine rather than masculine. Unfortunately, we seem to be on a path in New Zealand of making strapping, masculine Pinot Noir. They should really be graceful.

'You're looking for breeding when making Pinot. Something that reflects the season. I don't use enzymes. Enzymes are for making toilet bowl cleaners.

'I've done ten vintages so I have ten different wines, but not ten different styles. If I can't get that extra something into my Pinot Noir then I reduce the price, even when last year's was much more expensive. It's like choosing only boy jelly babies because they have that little extra bit.'

As well as Pinot Noir, Willie and Lea planted Syrah, Cabernet Sauvignon and inadvertently, a mystery grape Willie subsequently called Che-Syrah (Whatever will be, will be). Watering only to get the vines established, Willie made intensely flavoured wines that have been described as 'distinctive' and 'curiously impressive'.

The Browns also produced Mareth, a Cabernet/Che-Syrah blend, and several vintages of a port-style, brandied Pinot, called Après. The latter didn't always achieve the recognition Willie reckoned it deserved.

Willie Brown: 'We entered it in the Easter Show, but since they didn't know what category to put it in, they didn't taste it. But they didn't refund either the wine or the money. On another occasion we were accused of including stour [rotten] fruit, when it was the brandy they could taste. Old wine styles are not even recognised here, in some cases.'

Willie's winemaking methods were also traditional – or unorthodox, depending on how you looked at them.

Willie Brown: 'Reset [second set] bunches are a control for your acid level. Instead of using tartaric acid, etcetera for balance, I use the reset bunches. It might only be a hundred kilograms but that's enough to do my fiddling. I don't filter, either.'

Willie Brown died in 2002, after a long battle with cancer. The vineyard has been leased, but Lea still markets the remaining wine from their ten vintages.

Lea Brown: 'Willie would try anything! If you could put it in your mouth, he would try it. He came down here to make the wines he wanted, and if people didn't like them he would drink them all himself. And he certainly wasn't going to waste his time drinking a lot of whites.'

The late Willie Brown and friend.
Pam Ryan

'You're looking for breeding when making Pinot. Something that reflects the season. I don't use enzymes. Enzymes are for making toilet bowl cleaners.' Willie Brown

Stratford Wines

Strat Canning, Margrain and
Stratford. *Pam Ryan*

It's nearly the end of May. The cloud has hung low through an otherwise
pleasant day. Around dusk a little rain drips politely through the few leaves
still on the trees. The air is cool and clean with hints of leaf mould and
stone. Almost all the grapes are in. A few rows of botrytised Riesling shrivel
slowly under the remaining nets at Stratford vineyard. The rain settles it.
We'll pick tomorrow.

Snipping off the fruit is easy enough. Virtually no leaves remain, so the
bunches are visible. But the nets snag on every dried tendril, making for
irritatingly slow work. A stiff wind a few days ago blew off most of the fruit
– if you can call it fruit. Shrivelled clusters of raisins, the undersides a furry
mush, puff clouds of mould spores when touched. Some grapes are still
whole: a sickly, spotted apricot and gold colour, but they are few and far
between. In parts you can walk ten or twenty metres without picking more
than a teacup full.

Strat Canning: 'Riesling can stand a level of even the rotten, brown,
shitty looking stuff. It adds quite a dimension to the varietal wine. But if
you can get that to shrink and raisin up and any rot that doesn't split
the berries open can raisin then you can get some amazing flavours.
But you lose more than half. A lot of my Riesling has already fallen
on the ground so I'll never get to pick that. No doubt more will fall as
we take nets off. So you lose half your volume, and you get less than
half the juice you do out of fresh grapes.

'Botrytised wines can also be difficult wines to make. Very prone to oxidation. Botrytis excretes an enzyme called laccase that oxidises juice just like that. So if they get a chance to get air, and the laccase lasts into the bottle, they'll produce vinegar. These wines naturally have high levels of volatile acidity and there is a legal limit on that. It's part of the style but can be excessive.'

Whether he's organising vineyard pickers or heaving buckets of grapes around the winery, Strat Canning's quiet, rapid-fire speech never seems to dawdle; as if his mind remains unruffled by his exertions.

He tips the unsightly fruit into large, blue, plastic bins at the winery. The process today is pretty low-tech, but with only 600 or 700 kilograms in total, that's no hindrance. A little enzyme is sprinkled over each binful, then it's in with gumboots, squishing the desiccated, furry mess into a pulp reminiscent of Mum's Christmas cake mix. Then it's into the press, which is nearly full when we've finished.

There'll be no free-run juice from this lot, but after a few minutes of pressing, a dark brown syrup drips into the collecting tray.

Successive presses extract a clearer, amber-coloured juice, before a final viscous goo is wrung out. Wasps by the dozen are lured to a sticky death in the saccharine mire.

'Two hundred and eighty three litres. Not bad.' Strat muses. The last of the liquid reaches a staggering 52 brix, but once the whole tank is stirred up it settles at 48.5. The Stratford Noble Riesling is under way.

Strat and his wife, Carla Burns, tend three hectares of their own, but Strat's day job is full-time winemaker at Margrain Vineyard. Apart from the Riesling, the bulk of Stratford Vineyard is in Pinot Noir, becoming more preponderant as an initial hectare of Chardonnay is phased out.

Strat Canning: 'I worked for MAF on fisheries' research for ten years. Two or three of us came from MAF: Gary Voss, Steve Tarring and me. And of course there were others from scientific backgrounds, like Neil McCallum and Stan Chifney, and the Martinborough Vineyards DSIR [Department of Scientific and Industrial Research] connection. Probably as much as anything, the idea of wine and grapes sort of spread around the smoko rooms of those sorts of places, with people thinking it all sounded like a good idea. I think most people went into it imagining it was a marvellous romantic thing to do, and didn't use

Stratford Wines

Not easy to find, since Strat produces only 600 cases each vintage, but worth searching for and great value. Stratford barrel-fermented Chardonnay is up there with some of Martinborough's best. Strat's Pinot Noir is big, concentrated and worth cellaring.

their statistical and scientific training to weigh it all up. Otherwise they probably wouldn't have ever been here.

'When I decided to get into the industry, I began the Charles Sturt wine science degree course from Australia. That took six years while I was working up north. A degree at half speed. It was very good. It told me where to look for answers and what questions to ask. I was working at de Redcliffe with Mark Compton, who is very strong on technical aspects. We'd spend hours going over details, and I wouldn't have even known what to ask about if I hadn't been doing the course. So correspondence while on the job can be much better than a classroom degree.

'Then I worked four years at Palliser as vineyard manager. Absolutely invaluable experience. They're not two different jobs, though. It's a continuum. Hopefully the viticulturist will work really closely with the winemaker, with the same feel for how it should be done.

'We came here in 1990 because it seemed to be a good place to grow grapes. At that time we thought ten acres would be sufficient. Of course it isn't, and if we were to do it as a stand-alone thing it would have to be two or three times that size. We haven't made any expansionary moves and probably won't now. We've changed tack, and couldn't afford expansion anyway. But I've enjoyed immensely being at Margrain and find it very satisfying. But it's also satisfying to have my own vineyard's name on the bottles.'

Margrain Vineyard

Graham Margrain reclines on a comfortable settee. His wife, Daryl, kneels in front of the wood-burner with a mug of coffee. It's early Friday evening. They've not long arrived from their work week in Wellington, where they run a construction business, and they're warming up their weekend cottage. They could be set for a couple of days R & R, but they're not. Margrain Vineyard is their 'other' business.

Daryl Margrain: 'We were looking for something a bit different, and friends took us to a new vineyard they'd just discovered, Denis's at Gladstone Winery. Denis hadn't been going that long, but he was very enthusiastic and showed us all around, even though he didn't know us.

And we said, well if he can do it, we can do it. So we came over here three weeks later and bought a block of land. We had been looking for something for a while. We looked at all sorts of stuff: walnuts, pines, motels; but Denis just made this sound so fantastic – and it was, and it is.'

Graham Margrain: 'We sold all our toys and put the money into this. The launch became the cellars and winery. We enjoyed wine but we didn't know a hell of a lot about it. We'd just started going to wine clubs and tastings and things.'

Daryl Margrain: 'When we drove into Martinborough for the first time about ten years ago, there was one restaurant: the Zodiac, a great restaurant. We didn't have any wine for lunch so we had to hop across to the pub where all they had was Blue Rock, so we drank a Blue Rock Sauvignon Blanc with lunch. Right next to us at the restaurant was an American couple, who had a bottle of Ata Rangi, and they were saying how beautiful it was. They gave us a taste and said, this is the place to go. So after lunch we followed them back. Graham just idled the car up and said, "This is the place".

'I'd have to be honest, in the early days it was more for the business than the love of wine. That changed. The more we got to know about Martinborough and the wines coming out of the place, the more we thought: "This is us".

'If it hadn't have been for the Ata Rangis we wouldn't have been able to do this. In fact it was Clive who told us to buy this land. Olly Masters set the whole vineyard out. He worked for us part-time for two years. If you wanted to go for top quality, people here were very supportive. But if you just want to come and get in on the back of the Martinborough name and don't care about quality, I think you might have a worse time. People here have already put a lot into the branding of Martinborough, and they want it kept up. They all help each other, borrowing each other's gear. They are good people. We found that surprising coming from Wellington where the business fraternity are at each others throats all the time.'

Once Graham and Daryl had the bit between their teeth, there was no holding them back. In addition to their original four hectares, they bought a block on Dry River Road, south of the town, in 2000, and the next year

Margrain Wines

Strat Canning tailors all Margrain wines for cellaring. Pinot Noir is the flagship and particularly worth pursuing. The whites – and there are several: Chardonnay, Riesling, Pinot Gris, Chenin Blanc and Gewürztraminer – are characteristically concentrated and elegant even when young, and blossom beautifully with age.

acquired the original Chifney vineyard just across the road from their winery. They lease a further four hectares. Stan Chifney's beloved Cab Sav vines have been top-grafted to Pinot Noir, which will eventually account for 70 per cent of their planting. The Margrains also grow Chardonnay, Pinot Gris, Chenin Blanc, Gewürztraminer, Merlot and Riesling: quite a range for Martinborough. When everything comes on stream, the total crush will exceed 100 tonnes.

Stan's old winery, the region's first, is leased as a popular café, but the most distinctive feature of the vineyard is a line of 15 contemporary, balconied villas overlooking wetland and farm paddocks. These are referred

Margrain Villas. *Pam Ryan*

'And it's not just eight or ten years where you don't make a profit: it's eight or ten years where you have to keep putting money in.' Graham Margrain

to locally as the tupping sheds: for their stylish corrugated steel cladding, and discreet appeal to weekending couples.

Daryl Margrain: 'We went to Epernay, Champagne Valley, and stayed in villas overlooking the vines. We didn't think about it until we got back, and we were walking up that strip and saying, "What are we going to do here? Three rows of vines, no it's not worth it." Then we looked at each other and we thought: "Villas!" We travel a bit, so we asked ourselves, "What do we want?" and this is it. Didn't want a strip of motels. We started with four. Wasn't enough. Then eight. Now fifteen. We're into conferences now.'

Expansion hasn't all been plain sailing, though. The woolshed the Margrains converted into a conference centre was torched by an arsonist, which postponed plans for a new winery as the centre was rebuilt.

Despite their passion for the vineyard, Graham and Daryl continue to live in Wellington.

Graham Margrain: 'We could move over here, but we quite like fifty/fifty. The double life is good, and we have some great people who make it easy to run by remote control. They have to be good and so does the wine.

'When we came here the Pinot Noir was just making its mark. We agreed that it's a variety that you do properly or you don't bother. We didn't want to get into the cheap and nasty. Some new vineyards have been set up here, but have fallen by the wayside because of poor quality wine. Those people wanted to make their own but lacked expertise in both viticulture and wine-making. Some people also underestimate the time it takes to earn a profit. It's not three years. It's not five. It's probably eight or ten. And it's not just eight or ten years where you don't make a profit: it's eight or ten years where you have to keep putting money in.'

Gary Voss and Annette Atkins,
Voss Estate. *Pam Ryan*

Voss Estate

Gary Voss and Annette Atkins are two of the MAF scientific contingent that virtually drained the department in the late eighties, when they trooped across the Rimutakas to plant grapes. But unlike some new operators, scientific or not, Gary and Annette were acutely aware of the crucial need to hit all the bases to survive.

Gary Voss: 'Before I wrote the cheque out [for their land] I went and checked out the Met Service thing and got hold of the Soil and Climate study. We were in research. If you're going to spend that much time and money on anything, you have to be certain you're not doing it on a whim.

'Around here, you bump into someone like Neil McCallum and you'll find yourself discussing the latest scientific study on the Net, or academic texts: always science. There's a lot of romance and art in wine, but there's got to be good science too, especially in the viticulture. As a scientist you'd hope you'd apply some of the rigorous training you have. There's a lot of trialing done here even after ten years. We're always analysing things. We don't leave anything to chance. Pen and paper and spreadsheets are always brought out pretty quickly when we're discussing something.

'Then there is marketing. Several small boutique wineries have gone under around here. Nothing wrong with their wine. It was sales and marketing. If you haven't sold it, you shouldn't be picking it. I worked for a year with Eurowine the wine distributors, before we'd even picked our first grapes, because I wanted to see how the marketing side worked, and that was a real eye-opener.

'I talk to people who run wine shops in Wellington, and they are still constantly amazed at how someone will come in and say "I'm this new label and I've decided to let you sell my wine." The wine-growers are stunned when they are shown the door, because there is physically not enough space on the shelves. We were about the ninety-fifth registered winery in New Zealand. Now there are something like three hundred and ninety!'

Gary spent a year in Australia studying oenology, before working vintages at de Redcliffe and Ata Rangi. Then he says, the hard work really began.

Gary Voss: 'My brother and I lived in that little wooden shed over there while we planted during one of Martinborough's coldest winters. Then I built the winery and Annette and I lived in that for a year or two. The lounge had a tractor parked in it and we had barrels down one wall. That's actually grounds for divorce. Then when we started to sell wine we had to clear a corner of the lounge. Customers loved it.

'I don't like going to a cellar door and being served by someone who knows nothing about the wine. It's hard work after spending all week in the vineyard to spend your weekend selling. But if you want to take people with you, you have to put the time in. If we can't, if we are picking or something, then we won't open.

'I worked in dive teams in MAF, so I'm used to hard outdoor work, but this is the hardest I've ever done. There aren't many outfits of our size where there isn't at least some salary from somewhere else propping it up. We've just hired a full-time vineyard manager and full-time worker. Up till now we've done everything ourselves.'

Voss Estate Wines

Neck and neck at the head of the Voss Estate field are Pinot Noir and Chardonnay: consistent quality. Also look out for their Riesling, Sauvignon Blanc and Waihenga: a fruity Cab Sav/ Cab Franc/Syrah blend.

The first vines on Voss Estate were planted just after Stan Chifney won gold for his '86 Cabernet Sauvignon. So Gary and Annette had a dollar each way on Burgundy and Bordeaux, planting equal areas of Pinot Noir, Chardonnay and Bordeaux reds. Subsequent vintages, however, persuaded them to favour Pinot, and much of their Cab Sav has been top-grafted to Sauvignon Blanc, which accounts for ten per cent of their total. Latterly, they've expanded by leasing.

Gary Voss: 'We've picked up quite a few vineyards for managing or lease from people who came over from Wellington in summer and thought, "Growing vines: this is a nice thing to do." But after six or twelve months they realise it's back-breaking agricultural labouring most of it. So they've happily handed it over for lease.'

Annette Atkins: 'We're often also offered fruit, but we won't let any fruit into our winery that we haven't controlled in the vineyard. Some importers won't buy wine made from contract grapes. They need to sell the story, so we need to guarantee consistency of both supply and quality.

'Fifty per cent of our production is exported, and fifty per cent is domestic. We are planning expansion and that will have to be exported. We have too many markets for our size at the moment, but that's risk management. At the moment we can't satisfy the demand for any of those markets, which is a nice way to be.

'When we first came here, export wasn't heard of. In '88 when we planted the first vines, if someone had said "Your wine will be sold in restaurants in London, New York, Sydney and Amsterdam," we would have fallen over laughing. But they're there now. It gives you quite a buzz. New Zealand sends off beef to the States and it gets ground up into hamburgers or whatever, and people haven't the faintest idea what they are eating. Whereas a bottle of wine sits on a table and it's an identifiable part of someone's experience: normally a pleasurable experience. Who made it and where it comes from is part of that experience.'

'There's a lot of romance and art in wine,
but there's got to be good science too,
especially in the viticulture.'   Gary Voss

Christina Estate

In 1999, Christina Eagan bought Walker Estate, next door to Ata Rangi, and renamed it Christina Estate. She found over a third of the two hectare vineyard planted in a mysterious red grape, mistaken at first glance for Syrah. In fact the cuttings from which the Walker Estate vines originated had indeed been grown as Syrah. Propagated at Little Akaloa on Banks Peninsula, they couldn't be planted there because the local council feared a vineyard would unduly inhibit the ability of nearby farmers to spray. Lincoln University offered the foundlings to Clive Paton at Ata Rangi. Within a year, Clive realised they weren't actually Syrah, and instead christened the unusual, red-juiced variety Super Seibel. Seibel is the common name for many French hybrid vine varieties. Because it imparts rich colour, Clive included Super Seibel in his Célèbre blend, but the proportion was so small – around five per cent, that it didn't warrant mention on the label.

Apart from Ata Rangi and Walker Estate, Walnut Ridge, Te Kairanga, Muirlea, Murdoch James and Margrain among others, planted or inherited the variety. Proliferating around the town, it attracted more names than an errant puppy: names like Petit Syrah, Durif, and Pseudo Syrah. Genuinely believing it to be Syrah, Walker Estate entered the wine in the Air New Zealand awards, and won bronze and silver. Subsequent publicity, however, let the varietal cat out of the bag, and the wine was rebranded Notre Vigne (Our Wine). It remains the mainstay of Christina's range, and is now called Charisma.

Only one other vineyard, Murdoch James Estate, produces a pure Super Seibel wine. The vine itself produces high yields of large, handsome bunches of tight berries with fantastic colour, and good sugar, acid and pH levels. Charisma, matured in oak for 18 months, is a powerful, earthy, tannic dry red with intense colour.

But what is the mystery grape? Several European growers have checked it out, but have come to no definitive conclusion. Even DNA testing in Australia failed to provide a match. Opinions in Martinborough differ. The late Willie Brown fancied it could be a Hungarian village variety. Roger Fraser of Murdoch James is certain it's a stand-alone variety, while Clive Paton contends it's a hybrid with Teinturier in its pedigree. 'Dyer' in French, Teinturier refers to grapes with distinctive red flesh and juice. The jury is still out.

Burgundy or Pinot New Zealand?

The best known Martinborough Pinot Noir variety is a celebrated clone known as the Abel, Gumboot, or Ata Rangi clone. Malcolm Abel, with whom Clive Paton worked a couple of vintages at the now defunct Kumeu winery in the early eighties, was for a time a customs officer. During his tenure, a vine cutting was confiscated from an incoming traveller. Apparently the aspiring viticulturist had hopped the fence at Romanée-Conti, the famous Grand Cru of Vosne-Romanée, snipped the cutting, and hidden it in his gumboot. Malcolm snaffled the first vines out of quarantine. In due course, he passed their progeny to Ata Rangi, from where they spread all over Martinborough. Newer strains, like the acclaimed Dijon clones, have been imported since.

So, much of Martinborough's Pinot Noir is grown from exactly the same range of rootstocks that populate Burgundian vineyards. But that doesn't make the wine the same by any means. Do we want it to be? Should our Pinot Noir winemakers mimic traditional Burgundy, or ought they to strike out on a more independent line: seeking a distinctly vernacular style?

Derek Milne – Martinborough Vineyard: 'Early wine-tasting groups told us very clearly what international style represented. You can make wine with all the technical expertise you like, but if you don't know what you are aiming for and can't recognise it as high style or whatever, you are never going to produce it. Burgundy is what we are aiming at.

'For us, Pinot Noir was a deliberate, commercial judgement.

'Ever since Danny Schuster made St Helena Pinot Noir, it was obvious that if you had a similar climate to Burgundy, then you might be able to make Pinot Noir. And if you could make Pinot Noir well, you would be in the money, because you would be making a red wine which was one of the most expensive in the world and the hardest to duplicate.'

John Comerford – wine judge: 'We are not here to create New Zealand Burgundy. That's not what it's all about. We are endeavouring to express the varietal characters of Pinot Noir according to our various districts, climate, soils and terroirs. To get that expression, however, we have to use Burgundian techniques. For instance: pre-ferment maceration to extract colour; the use of indigenous yeast, rather than cultured though some prefer the control and aren't convinced there's a difference; sensitive handling post-fermentation: i.e. accepting the wine is fragile and protecting it. These are all standard Burgundian practices.

'There are still some people who do extended macerations as with Cabernet, but this tends to create a style that doesn't have the hedonistic aspects of what Pinot Noir is all about.

'New Zealand is more fruit varietal. It has a vitality that distinguishes it from Burgundy, and that's because of the elevated acidity all New Zealand wines tend to have. Burgundy has subdued fruit characters through the berry, cherry, plum spectrum, but they are not as assertive as ours. They tend to develop more savoury, mushroomy, forest floor characters much earlier than ours.

'I encourage diversity of style and exploration. I would rather appreciate what the vineyards are doing, than endeavour to lead them in particular directions. The success of Martinborough is that ten leading producers are producing quite different wine styles.

'However we can't say yet that our Pinot Noir has an ability to improve after ten years. We don't really know why yet. Could be vine age, high water tables, young soil structures.'

Oliver Masters – Ata Rangi: 'You can't make New Zealand Pinot Noir like Burgundy even if you try. So you are better to pursue the New Zealand potential. Burgundy will tend to be quite locked up and tight for the first few years. That's a more tannin-orientated, less uplifted fruit character than we produce.

'On the other hand, traditional Burgundy has been a great expression of fruit. Sauvignon Blanc had never been like that [in Europe]. So there's not the same potential to redefine the variety with Pinot Noir.

'All of that said, it's not always easy to tell the difference, even for those who should be experts.'

Kai Schubert – Schubert Wines: 'I attended the Steamboat Meeting in Oregon. That's the Pinot Noir winemaker workshop, where I met Neil McCallum.

'There was a lot of blind tasting going on. I was sitting next to a group of Burgundian winemakers, and they were so sure there was this one Grand Cru. Of course it wasn't Grand Cru. It was Dry River. There was Neil McCallum smiling away, and the French very upset.'

Filling the press.
Pam Ryan

The Pinot Noir, Chardonnay and Sauvignon Blanc are all strong and worth trying. Bubbly, and some different Pinot selections are on the way.

Alana Estate

Ian Smart is a focussed, no-nonsense sort of a chap. Once he and wife Alana, influenced by holidays in France, decided a vineyard was the business-lifestyle they wanted, he set out quite systematically to find the right spot. Not exactly an easy task, as they were in Britain at the time, where Ian was a builder-developer, Alana an air stewardess. The couple came home temporarily in 1993 and starting in Gisborne, Ian worked his way south, allowing a day or two in each area that interested him.

Ian Smart: 'I thought it was going to be Marlborough. I wasn't really that interested in staying in Martinborough even for the day I'd booked, but then I tasted some of the wine and thought, "This is pretty good". And it's close to Wellington. I did go to Marlborough, but all I could think about was what was happening here.

'I went to see Clive [Paton] that day and he helped me. He set me on the trail of this piece of land. I kept at the owner over two years until one day he just said, "Yes". We moved back in '95 and started planting as soon as possible.'

With just under twenty hectares of vines, Alana is one of the more substantial of the newer Martinborough vineyards. Sixty per cent is Pinot Noir, thirty per cent Chardonnay and ten per cent Sauvignon Blanc. Some Riesling was planted but has been taken out. Ian plans to concentrate on Pinot Noir, Chardonnay and 'a bit of fizzy'. But although his plot is way too large to be called a lifestyle block, Ian still prefers to do much of the work himself.

Ian Smart: 'I enjoy banging posts, running wires, the carpentry side and working outside. So fifty acres suits me fine.

'It's a good size to manage and promote. I did the financial numbers and fifty acres is about it. You can build top product without having too *much* product. I'm also not sure if you can maintain quality if you get much bigger than that. We jumped the output in lumps to manage the growth.

'In fact we're expanding the winery now. It's gravity fed, with the press at the top. We push the wine into barrels with CO_2 gas, and rarely use a pump. It definitely makes a difference, especially to Chardonnay.'

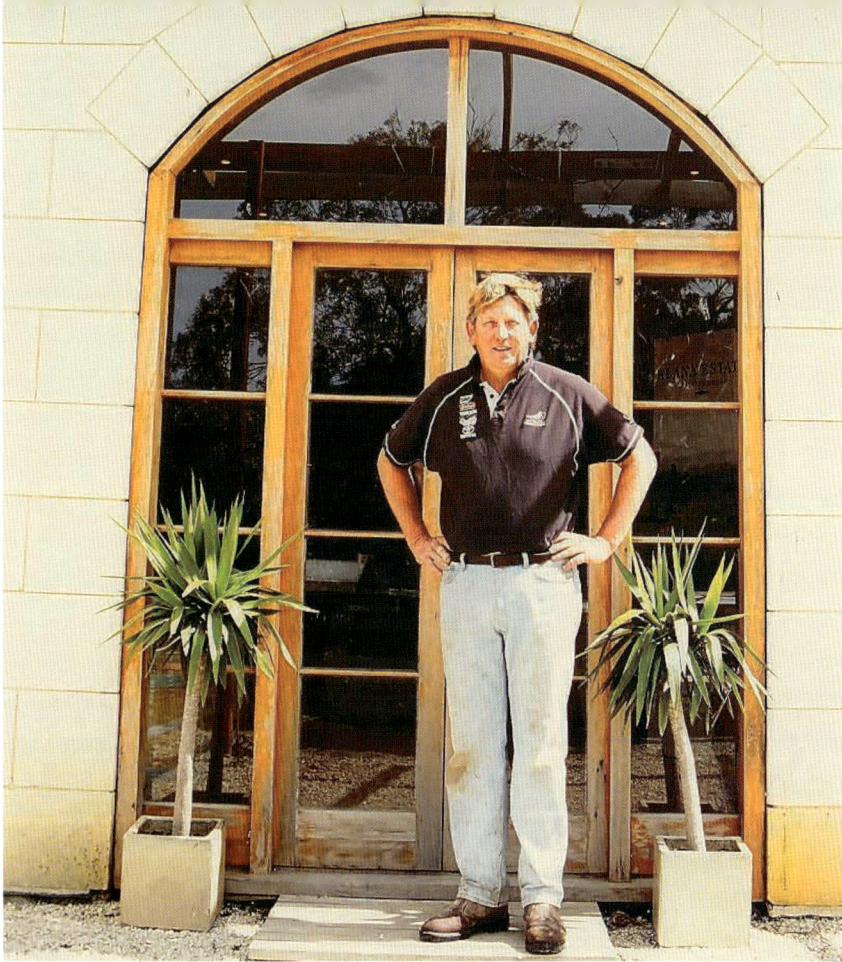

Ian Smart, Alana Estate. *Pam Ryan*

Ian is aiming Alana wine at the top of the market. It's a matter, he maintains, of believing in New Zealand's ability to produce top food and wine.

Ian Smart: 'We need to get the price up overseas. I always buy thirty-five pound Burgundies to compare them. We had a flash lunch in Burgundy and I took my '99 Pinot Noir. When they opened it I was very nervous. But as long as we get respect for good, New World-style Pinot, and we did, then I'm happy.

'New Zealand wines look great early on, but don't always cellar well. It's down to vine age. You can't expect five-year-old vines to produce twenty-year-old wines. We were lucky. When we planted in '95 we planted all Dijon clones. I'm aiming for a clonal selection.

'There's no point in producing European style wine. Sauvignon Blanc has already done it with difference. That's what we want: a point of difference.'

Stonecutter Vineyard

There's a brisk edge to Roger Pemberton's lunch appetite. He's spent the morning working on Stonecutter's new winery. He's built it himself from scratch, and he contemplates the next stage as he chomps into a mini smorgasbord of Vogel's bread, salami, cheese and tomatoes laid out on the kitchen bench. He made the bench, too: indeed he and partner Lucy Harper have pretty much hand built their entire spread: home, vineyard, winery, business and lifestyle.

Roger Pemberton: 'We bought the land seven years ago. It was basically a flat paddock with four willow trees, pittosporum planted front and back, and a deer shed. This house was an old shearers' quarters that we moved onto the property.

'We completely changed the way it was laid out: there were lots of dividing walls through it that we removed; we took off the original iron cladding and re-fixed it, and changed windows too. There are still additions I want to do, of course.'

Lucy Harper: 'What I didn't realise at the start was that a really strong motivation for Roger is a desire to physically make a mark: physically make things. So it's that totally Kiwi thing, "I do it myself", but on a bigger scale. He's not content with building a deck onto the house.'

Roger Pemberton: 'I find it much more interesting and satisfying than the office in that I can decide more or less what I do each day, and I don't have someone asking me to put together performance criteria for what I'm doing. There's also no time to be bored. There are always projects to get your head around. But then, I generate projects.

'We both have science backgrounds, we've both done chemistry, and are quite analytical and Lucy is a good gardener. But in terms of viticulture, we had no formal skills. We still use our scientific training: always checking the variables.'

A chance invitation to Clive Paton's fortieth birthday opened Roger's eyes to possibilities other than the bureaucratic grind. Recently redundant in the late eighties, he worked at Ata Rangi for a few weeks, and was smitten. Even another Wellington office job, albeit interesting, didn't cure the affliction.

Stonecutter Wines

The two Pinots, Gris and Noir, are available through mail order and on several Wellington and Auckland restaurant wine lists. Look out for Merlot and Topaz: a Sauvignon Blanc/ Gewürztraminer aperitif.

Far left:
Communal effort. *Pam Ryan*

Roger Pemberton: 'We would come over and visit Clive and Phyll, particularly at times like vintage, and I used to get pretty excited about the whole business of making the wine, and reluctant to leave. And every time, as we drove back over the hill, I'd say, "I'm not really ready to go home. I'd like to stay". In 1994, we'd just had kids and I was at a stage where I was really pulling at the traces and wanting to shift out of office stuff.'

Lucy Harper: 'I'm reluctant to move until I'm ready, but I could see that with two small children we needed a change. So I said, "Let's come over and see what it's like".'

Roger Pemberton: 'I got leave without pay, and in less than a year it was obvious I wasn't going back.

'We were not avid wine drinkers initially. I got hooked after being introduced to good Pinot Noir. I can remember one or two marvellous wines that I found. Layers on layers on layers that take you to a long, long, long finish that is truly amazing.

'In hindsight, we were optimistic in terms of the percentage of retail sales. We're looking at it again now. We should be able to make a decent living: not a huge living, and even that will rely on good prices. Up till now, we have been cautious about loading our plants up. We did ten tonnes last year and around eleven this year, heading up to sixteen or seventeen tonnes total. That's about two tonnes to the acre on average, across all varieties.'

Lucy Harper: 'The rationale behind our range is we plan a cellar door, so we needed more than just one variety. Roger liked the Merlot from around Martinborough. Likewise with the Gewürz, which is a very sweet aperitif, late harvest style.'

Roger Pemberton: 'One of the excitements is trying to convert the process of looking after vines to producing wine which is complex and flavourful, and that people will be happy to have an inch in the bottom of the glass, and just smell it or drink only a little, because it's so powerful, so complex, that you don't have to keep sipping and sipping.

'What we've done so far is rely on the quality of the grapes to produce good wine, quite successfully up till now. This block is looking to be a good one. But it's not just luck. It's also those many, many hours in the vineyard, and a lot of care and thought in the winery. We do everything.'

Walnut Ridge

Ex-pat American Bill Brink studied politics at Victoria University, but turned his back on academia and almost by chance, became a winemaker. His first wine, Walnut Ridge 1994 Pinot Noir, won a silver medal. In 1997 he won the Air New Zealand champion Pinot Noir trophy.

Bill Brink: 'From my early days at university I had a desire to learn about and drink wine, and did so over fifteen years. But that was the extent of it. When people ask me what I knew about the industry before I came here, I say, "I knew how to pull a cork".

'When I came here I drank Cabernet, and Chardonnay, and a little Sauvignon Blanc. Pinot Noir I'd never touch. "It's that thin, watery, lolly stuff": that's the perception you had of what locally produced Pinot Noir was about, and I don't think it was far off back in the late seventies, early eighties. Which is why I planted Cabernet. If I started over again now there's no way I'd put in Cabernet. In good years you can make a very good Cabernet, but not as consistently as with Pinot Noir. It became obvious very quickly, that if you were going to succeed at making wine in Martinborough, you'd have to do it with Pinot.

'Initially we came out here for a drive on a Labour Weekend in '86, and saw this place advertised in a dairy window in Featherston. We rang the real estate agent and said, "Show us two or three places". He showed us this place, and I thought, "Dry River on one side, Ata Rangi on the other. It's got to be a good spot". We put a ridiculously low offer in for this place, and a very high price on our place in Haitaitai. And it all happened within five days.

'Although grapes were in the back of my mind, the initial idea was to plant apricots and walnuts. I talked to Stan Chifney, the patriarch of winemakers here. He said there were too many grapes around. I shouldn't plant grapes. But I worked wineries and vineyards those first two years and realised grapes were where it was going to be.

'Certainly in those early years, as I watched people come over from Wellington every weekend, I realised places didn't have to spend a dollar on advertising if they chose not to. People were buying by the case. Vineyards were sold out after three or four months. And that looked pretty easy. Well, it did then.

'On top of that, things are quite handy this size. Your overheads are low, you do most of the work yourself, the business is rather simple, and with a good name you have no problem selling your wine. Life is sweet. Is there any advantage in being bigger? Our wine is different because Walnut Ridge is small. In summer after verasion [when the grapes change colour] we have the luxury of just going out for a walk in the evening with a pair of secateurs, and walking up and down a couple of rows: taking off shoulder bunches, taking off second set. If you had forty or fifty acres, you wouldn't do this. You just can't. So then when you pick the fruit, you can say to your people, "Just pick it". They don't have to sort it. You don't have to sort it when it comes into the winery either. It's already been done. And you would like to think that process, as opposed to machine-harvesting, will mean there's going to be a difference in the final product.

'At times I sit here and think, "Your whole life is consumed with this. It's all you ever talk about". I've never seen so many people who are so wound up in what they do. They are incredibly passionate about what they do. If I was not involved in it I'd say, "These people need to get a life".

'When I started I set out to make the best Pinot in New Zealand. Well, I've done that. And I think, "Now what?" I think maybe I could do something else. But there's nothing else I would like better.'

Bill Brink died in 2002. His vineyard, with the walnut trees he planted on the rise, has been bought by Ata Rangi.

Washing the barrels. *Suellen Boag*

'But it's not just luck. It's also those many, many hours in the vineyard, and a lot of care and thought in the winery. We do everything.' Roger Pemberton

Why Martinborough?

Steve Smith – Craggy Range Winery: 'Martinborough is *the* prestige wine region in country. It has the potential to make the greatest cool climate wines in the country. Possibly excluding Bordeaux varieties. The world will know about Marlborough, but those really in the know will know about Martinborough. Without a doubt the most exciting Sauvignon Blanc, the most exciting Riesling, the most exciting Chardonnay and the most exciting Pinot Noir in New Zealand have all come from Martinborough. I think Martinborough will always produce greater Pinot Noir than Marlborough will. I just get that sense.'

Claire Mulholland – Winemaker – Martinborough Vineyard: 'I've always been impressed by the wonderful consistency possible here. I have tasted a flight of several years from prominent vineyards. Even small vineyards here can turn out really good Pinot Noir.'

Why is Martinborough wine so good, even great, so often? How does the district manage to turn out such a range of varieties, in such quality, year after memorable year? How can so many vineyards – some almost microscopic in output, others comparative heavyweights – all achieve so highly?

Kai Schubert – Schubert Wines: 'We basically tasted the wines from every winery [in Martinborough] and there was not one bad one there. We thought there must be something right with the climate, because you need quality fruit to make good wine. The overall quality was so good we thought this must be holy ground sort of thing.

'There's a big diurnal range here. Dry, cool winters kill off bugs and the dryness discourages mildew and mould.'

Derek Milne – Martinborough Vineyard: 'It is a matter of where the grape has the heat to ripen in relation to the rainfall coming in late autumn or early winter. In that regard, Martinborough is most like Dijon, in northern Burgundy.'

Are those particular climatic parameters Derek Milne identified in the late 1970s all there is to it, or does Martinborough have other strings to its bow?

Neil McCallum – Dry River: 'We are lucky to have certain things. First, when rain comes to Martinborough, and it's a dry place, it normally comes on a southerly and it's cold. So it's very rare for rain to promote botrytis. Second: we get very consistent rainfall in autumn. We can rely on our autumns. Third: every three or four years, New Zealand gets a major tropical cyclone. It will ravage Auckland. It will come through and stop just that little bit north of here. We'll just get a decent dump of rain, but that's all. There are a lot of interplays of weather that never showed up on the stats, that we're just lucky to have.

'Fourth: Martinborough naturally crops low, which is best for the production of quality wine. If you have to drop fruit at verasion, [when grape colour changes from green to red] the wine is never quite as good as if it had naturally set the crop at the right level. We've done tests on it.'

Clive Paton – Ata Rangi: 'Because there was so much background science involved originally in choosing Martinborough, there's a rigorous intellectual backbone to the wine industry here. Also look at the background of many of the people who've set up here. Neil McCallum, Strat Canning, Stan Chifney, Roger Pemberton, Derek Milne, Gary Voss, Annette Atkins and Steve Tarring. For those people, sourcing of scientific information is second nature. And there is a lot of info now available that we have to read. When there are soil issues, underground water issues or whatever, we don't hesitate to use a scientist or a consultant.'

Steve Smith – Craggy Range: 'It's more a Pinot Noir community here. These people are nuts about it. It's the main reason they are here. That community character and the people who contribute to it, have a big effect on the way a region develops. That's the classic thing about terroir that people forget. It's not just soil and climate. It's culture as well. A combination of all three. That's an edge that Martinborough has.'

Chris Buring – Te Kairanga: 'The beaut thing about here is the balance. The wines have lovely acid. You can enjoy them in their youth, but they will cellar well too.'

John Comerford – wine judge: 'Martinborough overall does have a distinctive character. The Pinot Noir is more sturdy and structured in composition than that of other regions in New Zealand. They have addressed the yield issue here, with no more than two tonnes to the acre. The climate assists of course, and high winds reduce flowering. A lot of Pinot Noir is marginal economically, but Martinborough has vine age compared to other parts of New Zealand.'

Clive Paton – Ata Rangi: 'I'm nicely surprised at the position of Martinborough now. I don't see it going backwards, unless we got a string of very hot years. If there's global warming, there's a possibility that one day in fifty or a hundred years time, we might be too warm to do what we do now consistently. The best years here are the average years: average heat, average sunshine, that sort of thing. What I saw in 2000 was all those good Pinots sitting on wine shop shelves. Very few places can do that.'

Pam Ryan

The Ripples Spread

Very few viable, unplanted vineyard sites remain on the Martinborough town terraces. The few that do come on the market command premium prices. A block on Puruatanga Road sold for $100,000 a hectare in 2002, an eight-fold increase since the mid-eighties when the industry was still proving itself. Inevitably, then, newer entrants in the industry cast their land net wider.

South of Martinborough, several districts have emerged. The largest, closest and most concentrated is Te Muna, a river terrace formed by the Huangarua River, just a few kilometres out of town. Here, Larry McKenna has planted his new Escarpment Vineyard, the massive Craggy Range vineyard has gone in, and Jeff Barber has established the smaller Pond Paddock vineyard.

Te Muna Road Vineyard

Te Muna sheep farmer Ian Campbell has been playing around with grapes for some time.

Ian Campbell: 'It all started when they got going in Martinborough, and Wyatt Creech started with the Om Santi block. I asked him about grapes here, and he said, "It's no good out there. It's too wet". I said, "Hell, it's drier than in town!"

'I put in two acres, though I knew nothing about grapes. I'm a sheep farmer. I put in a mixture of Sauvignon Blanc, Chardonnay and Pinot. That two acres was just a trial. Everything went wrong – from possum damage to birds eating the fruit. There was nothing wrong with the grapes. It was more my lack of knowledge. And when I should have been doing the grapes I'd go and work on the farm. So it sort of trickled along and I sold the grapes to Palliser – the few that I got. Then I sold four twenty-five acre blocks to various people. When my son was home, he said, "Why not put in another ten acres?"

'It gets to a point where farming can't match the value of the land. And the only thing wrong with selling those four blocks – and I knew it would happen once I sold them – it really becomes hard to farm. So it gets to a point where you've really got to plant grapes or sell up. Because some times of the year you can't spray barley in the next paddock or whatever. I don't know if it will be in my lifetime, but all this road will be in grapes one day.

'I was pleased to buy clay land a few years ago. It was damp. While the stony stuff on the flat was always full of grass-grub and it only had grass in September/October. It's turned right round now.

'I might go into a joint venture with someone. There's another hundred and eighty acres down here. We'll see about that.'

One hundred and eighty acres is a lot of wine. Watch this space.

The Escarpment Vineyard

Larry McKenna touched down from Queenstown less than two hours ago. He frequently consults for Central Otago vineyards. On the drive back home from Wellington airport, he detours to a tiny, recently established vineyard near Masterton. The owner wants his advice. Larry is one of only a handful of Martinborough vineyard personalities with sufficient mana to be immediately identified in conversation by his first name, and his opinion and guidance are often sought. The first trained wine professional in the area, Larry forged Martinborough Vineyard's illustrious reputation over some dozen vintages.

Learning as he went – Larry had no experience with Pinot Noir before coming south from Delegats – he concentrated first on increasing fruit ripeness. No sooner had his trellising achieved that by enhancing sun exposure, than Larry switched his attention to the influence of oak barrels, and then to fermentation techniques. He pioneered experimentation with whole-bunch and whole-berry ferments, and extended skin maceration, visiting Burgundy to learn first-hand. New Zealand's first full-bodied, multi-layered Pinot Noirs were the result, so different from their light, one-dimensional progenitors.

John Comerford – wine judge: 'In '89, Larry got five trophies. He gained international recognition and was the first New Zealander invited to Oregon. He has made an unsurpassed contribution to the development of our Pinot Noir.'

Larry McKenna, Escarpment Vineyard. *Pam Ryan*

Escarpment Wines

Larry's first vintages under his new label, a Pinot Gris and Pinot Noir, were made from contract-grown fruit, from the Martinborough district. They are both exceptional.

Derek Milne – Martinborough Vineyard: 'He is obviously an exceptional winemaker, but Larry had two other great attributes. He was very good at promoting himself and his wines. He appealed to opinion leaders like Oz Clark, because he was right up front, rough-hewn, no bullshit. Larry's other great strength was being able to work in less than ideal conditions, with less than ideal equipment.'

Larry McKenna: 'At Martinborough Vineyard, I couldn't afford to get Saatchis to market for us. So I had to just get on my bike. I'd never done it before, and I didn't know what I was doing. I'd front up there and just talk about it. Apparently it was very successful. People enjoyed that approach. I don't know whether it was original but it was all I knew how to do. I was never trained in marketing bullshit. I just cut through a lot of the crap and gave them the facts.'

Larry left behind twenty-year-old vines at Martinborough Vineyard, but took with him a towering reputation, and formidable experience and drive. And he had his name.

Larry McKenna: 'Anyone can grow it. Anyone can make it. Anyone can pack it and put it out in the shop here. But turning it into money: that's the trick. It made life easier knowing we had some sort of brand, some sort of position. The brand was McKenna, Pinot Noir and Martinborough. We stuck with all those.'

Escarpment Vineyard's twenty-two hectares are now planted. Within three years the vineyard will produce 15,000 cases: over two thirds Pinot Noir; the rest Chardonnay, Pinot Gris, Riesling and Pinot Blanc.

Larry McKenna: 'I knew when I left Martinborough Vineyard, that I was starting all over again with a young vines. So I've put a lot of thought into creating old fruit out of a young vineyard. I'll tell you if I've learnt anything in a year or two.'

Pond Paddock Vineyard

Jeff Barber had quite a wine cellar at home in Canada. He sold it, before he moved out to New Zealand.

Jeff Barber: 'Thing is, the guy who bought it from me has sold it on – at a profit! Selling up was hard, but since then, the learning curve has grown steeper. The vineyard has proved to be more work than we thought. We thought we'd run a B&B as well. Well no way with two small kids *and* a vineyard.'

A victim of its own success, perhaps, the Martinborough wine industry has developed a few growing pains.

Jeff Barber: 'There's more vineyard planted at Te Muna now than around Martinborough itself. And as the vineyards boom, it gets harder to find people to do things. A lot of service people are over-committed. The worst part is staffing. It's difficult to find workers. People often don't show up when they promise. If it's a cold day or a wet day, we figure that half the people won't come in.'

Jeff and Kiwi wife, Christine, bought their block of land in 1996, built their new home, then in 2000 planted four-and-a-half hectares of Pinot and a third as much again in Chardonnay and Riesling.

Jeff Barber: 'I used to drink a bit of Saintsbury from California, and some from British Columbia. But I didn't flip over it. We're growing Pinot here because that's the one. I'd probably drink Cabernet from preference. Around the house we have about four hundred and fifty plants of Cabernet, Merlot and Cab Franc. I would have gone for a more Bordeaux style, but when I came here, I quickly realised that if I grew all, say, Cabernet, I would crop at about the same levels as Pinot Noir, but I would get maybe fifteen dollars less a bottle for the wine. So Pinot is the best thing for here. Anyway, to try and compete with the huge number of places that make good Bordeaux-type reds, to me is too hard a job. The Pinot world is a bit different from the Cabernet world, because not everywhere can you make good Pinot. Here, you can.'

Vine prunings. *Pam Ryan*

'It's very, very, very special land … there's
something different about Martinborough
and its soils. The rocks are different; we
don't know why.' Steve Smith

Craggy Range Winery

Steve Smith is into rocks in a big way. Not so much the rocks themselves, as their influence on his wine: and Steve knows a lot about wine. He gained his Master of Wine in 1996. As he strides around the largest vineyard in the Wairarapa, his enthusiasm for the place, its different soil compositions, and the wine that springs from them, bubbles out of him. Smashing a couple of rocks together, he breaks one open, and eulogises what's exposed inside.

Steve Smith: 'These weathered products that come out of rocks are a little like tonics for vines. They are very complex minerals. See, the roots go where they are sent. They delve into rocks looking for minerals. There's some pretty cool stuff happening in there. See all the roots in there? They're weathering to clay. That's full of goodies, that stuff. It's very, very, very special land.'

Steve has worked in most areas of the industry: phyloxera studies, post-graduate work in the Napa Valley; research with prominent viticulturist Dr Richard Smart; as group viticulturist at Villa Maria – then into strategic wine-making and international marketing. He's combined his extensive expertise with the financial backing of American-Australian businessman Terry Peabody, who has invested some $65 million in the label.

Craggy Range was initially established in Hawkes Bay, where Steve led the charge in establishing the Gimblett Gravels district brand. The company focuses on single vineyard wines: Bordeaux varieties and Chardonnay in Hawkes Bay, Pinot Noir, Sauvignon Blanc, Chardonnay and Riesling at Te Muna. The vineyard is split into distinct planting blocks.

Steve Smith: 'There are eight different blocks of Sauvignon Blanc on forty hectares down here. Each block has a different amount of stone that produces different characters. So we ferment them separately, and then put a blend together that we think best represents that particular vineyard.

'Thirteen thousand to fifteen thousand years ago, the river retreated and left the river terrace exposed. Geologically it's the same terrace as in the vineyards in town known as the soils of the Martinborough Terrace.

'These soils down here on this lower terrace, are much younger,

Craggy Range

Steve has great faith in the Martinborough area for quality Sauvignon Blanc, and that's the only wine produced so far from this vineyard. All indications are it could be a stunner. A vineyard to watch.

laid down in the ensuing ten thousand years, and are almost identical to what you get in Wairau Valley in Marlborough. Not so weathered as on the top terrace, and not much clay. The unique aspect of this soil is that about ten per cent of the stones are limestone. As far as I am aware there is no other rocky alluvial soil in New Zealand that has limestone amongst it. There are vineyards with limestone but it doesn't tend to be alluvial. We didn't know that when we bought the property. So it was quite exciting when we dug those holes. We are finding characters in the first crop from the bottom terrace that are distinctly different from the rest of the vineyard.

'We spent a year coming down here [to Martinborough] with a soil specialist and talking to farmers in pubs over many weekends, all over the Wairarapa. There's something different about Martinborough and its soils. The rocks are different; we don't know why.

'Later we came back and asked, "Are there parcels of land that haven't been developed as vineyards?" We got aerial photographs, overlaid soil maps. Where soil maps were wrong, we dug holes in people's vineyards and sides of roads, in the early mornings, to see what was there.

'It became clear that the one area that hadn't been developed was Te Muna Road. So we spent a lot of time talking to the owner of this land about soil, climate etc. By its elevation we predicted slightly later ripening than in town and more extreme conditions: hotter, windier. That proved correct.

'After three years' experience we have found that over a season the GDDs [Growing Degree Days – a measure of accumulated temperature over a year] on Te Muna Road are the same as in town. Spring and early summer are cooler, and mid-summer and autumn are warmer. That's consistent with slightly higher altitude areas, where you have a slower start to the year, then once you settle in, it stays hotter longer.'

Given Steve's drive, expertise and enthusiasm, it's not difficult to see why he's such a forceful and tenacious protagonist in the Martinborough Terrace Appellation dispute. (The original appellation would prevent Craggy Range from using the term "Martinborough Terrace" on their labels.) Those same qualities undoubtedly attracted Terry Peabody.

Steve Smith: 'My great ambition has always been to make single vineyard wine on small parcels under my own label. I had just started doing

Autumn petticoats. *Pam Ryan*

that while working at Villa Maria, when Terry Peabody called me from the other side of world, and said his family was interested in getting involved in wine. He had built up numerous businesses and then sold them, but wanted something for his family and posterity. According to his wife and daughter, he would not be allowed to sell or take money from a wine business. He had been in France and asked Baron Rothschild, where he should set up. The baron said "Go to New Zealand".

'He rang me up already knowing more about me than I did, and asked me to help find him some land. We tendered for Gimblett Gravels land and got it. Eventually we spent time together in '98 and he said "I know you want to do your own thing but why don't you do your own thing with us?" It's turned out to be a fantastic combination of resources. Neither of us could have done what we've done without each other.'

Station Bush Vineyard

Barbara Smith is well connected in the wine business. Her mother was a Beetham, and Larry McKenna uses her grapes for his superb Escarpment Pinot Gris. She and Larry go back a fair way. They both started at Martinborough Vineyard in 1986. Barbara wanted to learn about viticulture, then plant a river flat on the family farm, up the Ruamahanga River north of town. An empty nest, with her youngest kids off at boarding school, had her fidgeting for something to do.

Barbara planted two-and-a-half hectares of Pinot Noir, Riesling and Sauvignon Blanc in 1988. Then ten years later, when Martinborough Vineyard decided not to continue with Pinot Gris, Barbara bought their new grafted vines. She had seen the response to the variety when working in cellar sales. However, much as she likes the white, Pinot Noir is still her pick.

Barbara Smith: 'It is absolutely magical. I like the complexity of ripe fruit in oak. But it has to be a big one. I like Clive's. I like Larry's. Those few top winemakers seem to be able to make good wine out of most fruit.

'Our vineyard is quite vigorous, with Ruamahanga River loam, and it floods occasionally, so it's not suited to big red varieties. Grafted rootstock helps holds the vigour back. However, we've been approached to put some ground into Shiraz. The reflection from that shingle hillside heats up the vines. We've gone to fewer but bigger vines to stress them and reduce vigour. With more than fifty buds per vine, we really load them up.

'Burnt Spur take everything except our Gris. The most important thing as a grower is to grow what the buying company wants. At the moment I'm following two different viticultural systems. I manage, and do a lot of pruning, and my son (and Larry's team sometimes) do all the tractor work and spraying.'

Barbara's involvement with grapes (if you don't count the Beethams) spans seventeen years, making her an industry old hand. Those early years of effort, she thinks, laid the foundations for Martinborough's current prosperity.

Barbara Smith: 'Being at Martinborough Vineyard was really exciting through that time. The industry was small and carried along by a few special people. Stan was a real character, Larry was laid-back, and of course Neil McCallum and Clive worked incredibly hard. If it hadn't been for those four it wouldn't have been as successful as it is.'

Burnt Spur Martinborough

Fifty-two hectares of vines is a substantial planting. But Burnt Spur Martinborough is not yet a household name, because the company is the latest incarnation of what began as Lintz Estate. Lintz became mired in a medal scandal in 1998. In the fall-out, the company underwent a major management and shareholding re-shuffle. Now back on track under CEO Stephanie Hagen, and guided by eminent winemaker Sam Weaver, Burnt Spur is aiming squarely at the export and top drawer restaurant trades.

Stephanie Hagen: 'In five years, we will be one of Martinborough's largest premium Pinot Noir producers. We'll also be making top Pinot Gris and Sauvignon Blanc.

'There is a criticism that Martinborough wine is overpriced, but it all sells, so it can't be. We do not wish to be overexposed in New Zealand, and want to be evenly spread around the world. We are focussing on the UK and US and then Japan. All three show considerable potential.'

Burnt Spur is ambitious and pioneering. Their largest planting is on largely clay soils at Fraters Road a few kilometres south-east of Martinborough. Received opinion locally holds that free-draining gravels, like those on the Martinborough Terrace where Burnt Spur also has plantings, are a must for Pinot Noir. However, there are precedents elsewhere: like Neudorf at Upper Moutere near Nelson, and the Fromm Clayvin vineyard in Marlborough. Both produce exceptional Pinot from heavier soils.

Perhaps not coincidentally, Stephanie previously worked as business manager for Huia, a Marlborough vineyard with a reputation for doing things just a bit differently. She notes the differences she's observed between the Marlborough industry and Martinborough.

Plunging Pinot Noir. *Suellen Boag*

Stephanie Hagen: 'Marlborough is further down the track in terms of industry development. It's much more market-driven there. Here it is producer-driven still. There's also a huge range of sizes of enterprises here. Some people are more backyard lifestylers. So production costs are higher than in Marlborough. Land was not so expensive here, but on the terraces it has certainly caught up with premium Marlborough sales, though cropping weights are lower.

'But there's more land available than some people would like to admit. There are huge tracts towards Masterton. Some other potential vine land is not flat, and would require more intensive labour inputs, and there is a labour shortage.

'The region is not as mechanised as Marlborough, nor does it have the critical mass for a wider range of services. So the support infrastructure is not as good yet. But it's coming.'

Burnt Spur's planning is firmly focussed on lifting production and quality. There's potential in the tourism market, perhaps even a restaurant, Stephanie acknowledges. But that will have to wait.

Stephanie Hagen: 'We need to be clear about exactly what our job here is, and we are well on the way.'

Coney Wines

Take the road to Lake Ferry and turn onto Dry River Road. The first vineyard you'll come to, behind a belt of pine trees on your left, produces a trio of wines of lyric note. Not only have Tim and Margaret Coney named their wines Ragtime Riesling, Rallentando Riesling and Pizzicato Pinot Noir, but Tim has also penned a poem on the back of each label. Not bad for a man who spent seventeen years in the calculating confines of the foreign exchange industry.

Coney wines tend to the dry side, not something you can say about Tim.

Tim Coney: 'I'm not a very practical person. In this game you need to be a bit of a plumber, a bit of an electrician, a bit of a mechanic, and I'm pretty ordinary, even awful, at those things. Which means if I'm fixing a hose, the first thing that happens is I disconnect it with the pressure full on and get a blast right up my mush. That's my starting point. I'm fully drenched at eight-thirty in the morning.'

And it's not certain that Tim actually planned his entry into the wine business.

Tim Coney: 'We were familiar with the Wairarapa, having brought our four kids over here a lot when they were younger. Margaret had sold her sports gear recycling shop and was looking for a new project. She bought a heritage building in Martinborough – it was probably best suited to a D9 demolition job – and was all set to spend the next two years restoring it as one of the first B&Bs here. I didn't want to be scraping off a hundred years of gunk and Margaret certainly didn't want me under her feet complaining, so I was trundled off to an auction one day, found someone pushing my hand up, and there we were: we'd bought our paddock.'

For four years Margaret ran her B&B, while Tim established the vineyard. Both had jobs in Wellington as well.

Tim Coney: 'It's a little fretful, because you get behind. We didn't want to be absentee operators. The whole point was to discover the pitfalls

Coney Wines

Tim's trio have all been well received in competitions, and are all worth a try. Pinot Gris and Syrah on the way.

first-hand. Why hand it over to a bunch of third parties and pay them? All those choices about which clones and which rootstocks, the density of your plantings, whether you have Scott Henry or whether you use vertical shoot positioning. All those things we'd done our reading on, asked the locals' advice, and made up our minds about: I wanted to do them.

'Locals are chary of Wellingtonians coming over here with their cheque books. But if you get stuck in and do the work yourself they will give you lots of support. It's not a recipe for becoming wealthy. You've only got to look around Martinborough. Even the successful owners of smaller, family-type vineyards still have '55 Holdens in the drive. We'll be happy if it looks after itself and pays for some victuals.'

From left Debbie Christensen, Tim and Margaret Coney, Coney Wines.
Pam Ryan

Murdoch James Estate

Murdoch James kicked off in 1986, with the two-and-a-half hectare Saleyards block next door to Ata Rangi, in the centre of Martinborough. While owners Roger and Jill Fraser lived in Melbourne, Clive and Phyll at Ata Rangi made their wine. In 1998 the Frasers bought Blue Rock Vineyard on Dry River Road, and shortly thereafter returned to live in New Zealand. Now their total planting tops 20 hectares, and the enterprise has become more and more a family affair. The estate is named for Roger's father, Murdoch James Fraser. Roger and Jill's son, Carl, works with them. Jill's sister, Barbara Turner is viticulturist, and Barbara's partner, James Walker is winemaker.

The Saleyards block is planted in Pinot Noir and Syrah. So too are the terraces at Blue Rock, as well as a diverse mix of Chardonnay, Riesling, Cabernet Franc, Pinot Gris, Merlot and Cabernet Sauvignon. Over a dozen different wines are produced each vintage, largely to satisfy visitors and guests at the splendid Murdoch James tasting room/cellar/café/function room complex.

Roger Fraser: 'We try and give people a good wine experience, even where they don't know anything about wine. We want to offer a total package: the best vineyard experience in the country.'

The varietal range also facilitates the Murdoch James core philosophy of organic polyculture.

Roger Fraser: 'Polyculture is similar to permaculture. You look for other things to interact with your principal crop to support it. We use animals for grazing, for fertiliser, and to clean up pasture in vineyards, and we use the surrounding environment to encourage more nectar-bearing plants to encourage predators of noxious insects.

'We have applied for BioGro certification and are currently registered as "in conversion." This is a good site to implement an organic regime, because of its isolation from neighbours. No one is spraying over the fence. Along the river boundary we have a lot of non-vineyard areas, and some natives. We're doing the town site as well. We are lucky to be next to Ata Rangi, who are very environmentally aware in their structures anyway.'

Murdoch James Wines

In the large range the Reserve Chardonnay and Fraser Pinot Noir stand out. The Cabernet Franc is also worth a try. Alternatively, visit Murdoch James and taste the lot.

James Walker: 'An organic regime is far less stressful than a conventional one. I used to have real problems dealing with MRLs [Minimum Residue Levels] and making sure my timings were right. Now no MRLs at all. We always had a "no residue" policy anyway. We found we had to. The export entry rules are getting tighter and tighter, with different countries having all sorts of different regulations.'

Roger Fraser: 'We made this change because it's right for the vineyard, rather than because it was a commercial imperative. But it's been amazing the amount of interest it has generated, for instance at the cellar door, and the enquiries we've had for export sales. As soon as I mention our organic regime, we get a lot of interest, even with existing customers. The guy who takes a huge proportion of our wine in Japan: I didn't think he'd be that fussed. He was thrilled. Obviously it's an important issue to people. More important than the amount of discussion it gets. New Zealanders don't know what they have.

'The essence of it is sustainability. We produce this product with no detriment to the land or to any people. We think that's a big accomplishment.'

As soon as I mention our organic regime, we get a lot of interest, even with existing customers.' Roger Fraser

Martinborough Transformed

Ten-fifteen, Saturday morning August. Out-of-town visitors are fixing breakfast in dozens of weekend bijou cottages around town. A lycra-clad jogger and her dog ruffle the dew along Puruatanga Road.

BMWs, Mercedes, and gleaming off-roaders that never do, line Kitchener Street. A muddy ute has to double park while its owner fetches his mail and a paper from the dairy. Neatly scissored ladies in fine Merino tops sip coffee in Café Medici or the Wine Centre across the road. Their partners browse the *Dominion* or real estate office windows. Between customers, Bruce Congalton sets out fresh cheeses in his corner shop: Taste of Martinborough. As gift and fashion shop doors swing open, the town is building to the weekend buzz it seldom has on weekdays.

This is an utterly different place to the town the first grape growers slipped into 25 years ago.

Duncan Milne: 'Martinborough was like any other New Zealand country town then. In the public bar of the pub you could buy anything: a fight, marijuana or a bit of the other. The rooms were like shearers' quarters.'

Larry McKenna: 'There were two pubs, neither of which you'd want to drink in, two take-aways and a motel. That was it.'

Daryl Margrain: 'When we first came, the whole town was fairly ramshackle. The hotel was unbelievable. We stayed there. People from the public bar had free and drunken run of the place. The beds were saggy wire-wove. Toilets down the corridor. It was like going back in time.'

But as local wine forged a reputation, Wellingtonians discovered Martinborough. Victorian cottages and villas were snapped up for weekenders and then B&Bs. Prices spiralled and local owners cashed up and moved to Featherston or Carterton. Such is the tourist appeal of the area, there are now over 800 tourist beds in the South Wairarapa.

Kitchener Street and the Square, the town centre, have metamorphosed into a slice of downtown Wellington in the country. The Martinborough Hotel's upgrade and expansion epitomises the transformation. Martinborough can thank expat Englishman Mike Laven, and his Kiwi wife, Sally, for that. As Mike sips coffee in the warm, welcoming corner bar of his hotel, it's difficult to imagine one person driving so many changes and developments in less than ten years. As he speaks however, his quiet, intense enthusiasm evinces a formidable energy.

Mike Laven: 'I was in property in Hong Kong. We started coming down to see Sally's parents from about '87, when we met. They had semi-retired near here. Every time we stayed it was Christmas or New Year. The rest of family were often there too, and it could be fairly crowded. So in 1991 we bought a house. We renovated it quite simply and Sally's parents looked after it and rented it out over weekends to cover rates etcetera. There were already a couple of other places for rent, but not much. We kept an eye on the visitors' book. Visitors went from being once a month, to once a week, and then even more frequently. So we became more interested in Martinborough and why this was happening.

'We got to know people like Larry and Sue McKenna and became more interested in Pinot Noir. We began to drink it in Hong Kong, and

Left:
Kitchener Street, Martinborough.
Pam Ryan

Right:
Martinborough Hotel. *David Wall*

became aware when Martinborough was written about in newspapers. For instance, Jancis Robinson writing about Martinborough wines in the *Financial Times.* We knew the reality of the town, and it was a place we didn't want to hang around in. Nothing happening here. The strange thing was though, the wine from here was being written about in the most respected newspapers. And in London, Martinborough wine was for sale in Oddbins for twelve pounds, thirteen pounds a bottle: right at the top of the range. People knew it was great wine. So we became more and more interested in this gap between the perception of this place around the world, and the reality that we knew.

Mike and Sally Laven,
Martinborough Hotel.
Pam Ryan

'There was bit of activity out in the vineyards but actually nothing happening in the middle of town. And at the same time, people were coming over here and staying at our place. So there was some sort of attraction. We drifted into this, really.

'In 1995, we had dinner with Larry and Sue and the subject of the hotel came up. The lease was for sale. We talked about what we'd do if we bought it. We talked to the real estate agent and indicated that if the freehold were for sale, we'd be interested. It is the best site in town. If Martinborough developed you couldn't go wrong here. Everything we did was done with gut feeling and incredible naivety. It's only an hour from Wellington, and once we started looking at Martinborough, we realised what it had. The Square is very unusual in New Zealand terms.

'I'd only been into the hotel loo before. The bar was pretty rough. The bank manager said "You must be mad, the last time I was in there I was beaten up!" We renovated and then added on, because specialist wine groups needed more than eleven rooms. There are sixteen rooms now.'

Mike and Sally moved back to Martinborough permanently in 1997 to keep an eye on their hotel. Not content with one project, Mike had the old Station House moved from Masterton and set up across the road in 1998–99. Then he developed the Wine Centre.

Mike Laven: 'We stole the idea [for the Wine Centre] from Margaret River especially, and Napa Valley. It's really a wine information centre, and a first in New Zealand. It's kind of an obvious idea. Cellar door sales in Martinborough are relatively small. Often vineyards are closed, anyway, when people visit.

'The first year was hard, as was the first year with the hotel. But the hotel gave the town the final push to develop. It changes perceptions of the place.'

However, change is rarely painless, and not everyone in Martinborough has been so enamoured of the vineyards and what they brought in their train.

'I firmly believe that the wine industry is like a three-legged stool. You have the vineyard, the winery and the marketing. If you let one go, the stool is going to fall over.'   Christine Kernohan

Clive Paton: 'Martinborough was very much a dying town. You couldn't get a pie or even petrol in the weekends. But after the vineyards developed, there was a split in the town. The older town was not interested in what was happening. They couldn't see that there'd be a future for their kids, that they wouldn't have to be a rousy or a fencer, or disappear.'

John Comerford: 'Vineyards came to the town and provided prosperity. But Martinborough is unique in that there is nowhere else in New Zealand where vineyards are so close to a town. So helicopters [for frost-fighting], spraying, bangers [to deter birds] have quite an effect. There was quite a bit of feeling that delayed implementation of the District Plan. 'Right to farm' issues arose, and a corridor was built into the District Plan preserving the right to continue viticultural practices. Even then, netting has had to take over from bangers.'

Left:
Martinborough
Wine Centre.
Pam Ryan

Right:
Martinborough
Museum.
Pam Ryan

135

Up the River

Just over a hundred years ago, the first Wairarapa wine was produced around Masterton. Some 70 years after those early vines disappeared, Martinborough got the jump on the rest of the region, re-established the industry, and set off a wine rush. That is inexorably spreading, as contract growers, viticulturists and winemakers explore and colonise new territory. The Martinborough experience is invaluable of course. It can tell growers considering areas outside Martinborough, what particular grape varieties require to flourish, and which soil profiles and climatic parameters to seek. Hardly surprisingly, soil types very similar to the river-cut gravel terraces around Martinborough are found up the Ruamahanga and Waingawa Rivers towards Masterton.

Christine Kernohan – Gladstone Vineyard: 'In ten years' time I'd be very surprised if it's not grapes from Opaki to Martinborough.'

Larry McKenna – Escarpment Vineyard: 'Martinborough is considered the jewel in the crown [of the Wairarapa]. But the reasons are that it got going first, most of the industry is here, and it creates the publicity with Toast Martinborough. But it's just further down the track.

'I'm very excited about the Mebus boys' site on Dakins Road.

'And if you look at the soil map of Gladstone, there's an area of soil just like here. It's also got the same circular rainfall pattern around it. So identical parameters climate-wise and soil-wise to Martinborough. I'm not so sure about north of Masterton. We'll see.'

Clive Paton – Ati Rangi: 'Wairarapa is an old inlet that's filled up with alluvial gravels. So much of it is good. There are huge areas on the Greytown Tauherenikau Plains where you might get seven good years out of ten compared with nine here [in Martinborough]. But in the scheme of things that's pretty good. You compare that with Burgundy or Bordeaux – that's still quite good.'

Gladstone, Dakins Road and East Taratahi

Gladstone Vineyard

Down the drive set about with birches, conifers and gums; around the expansive pond of ducks and geese; on past the imposing, white, two-storey colonial house, layered top and bottom with verandas, then up to the winery itself: dormers, fresh cream weatherboards, and barn-red roof. All in all, Gladstone offers a comprehensive sense of arrival.

That's intentional. Owners Christine and David Kernohan don't just want to grow and make wine. They want visitors: lots of them.

Christine Kernohan: 'People were coming to Martinborough, but not anywhere near us. We wanted to make this a destination. So we set up the café in our first year. It's part of the marketing. Our daughter and a friend ran it doing platters and the like. There are a lot more cafés in the Wairarapa since we started but still not many at vineyards.

'We are getting more people down from Auckland, even Palmerston North; and people are driving from Hawkes Bay to Wellington this way now, when they didn't before.

'It would be nice to have a real wine trail up here. It's a wee bit like car yards: you go where there's more than one. We need more than just us and Jon [Fairmont Estate] next door. I'd love to see a real tourist scenic trail. You'd come down from Opaki, into Mebus and Borthwick, have a picnic by the cliffs, then down here to Gladstone. Then you could head on down to Martinborough. The place will only succeed when we all pull together.'

Christine and David bought Gladstone in 1996 from Dennis Roberts and Richard Stone, who had established the vineyard ten years earlier.

Through the press. *Suellen Boag*

Roberts turned out some classy wines, so Christine had a solid reputation to build on.

Christine Kernohan: 'We hired a winemaker, Jean Charles Van Hove. I was basically his cellarhand for that first year. He had spent time with Corbans and then Montana. He was a great guy to work with. I was very lucky with him. He was a great teacher. We had very good wines that first year. I've done quite a bit of course work since then, and picked a few people's brains.

'It certainly was a learning curve. Fortunately I like learning. I have a science background, not quite the right sciences, but it's been good getting down that track, and I've always enjoyed wine.

'I was looking for another business in the rural sector. We had been in a farming venture, which we were getting out of, when this place became available. We weren't particularly looking. It was very much the right place at the right time.

'We took a great leap forward when we started to put our team together, too. Especially Spencer Southey' my vineyard manager.

'I firmly believe that the wine industry is like a three-legged stool. You have the vineyard, the winery and the marketing. If you let one go, the stool is going to fall over. So I took the decision to focus on the winery and the marketing management. Spencer focuses on the vineyard, but we work as a team in the winery, too. It's enabled us to go forward.'

Gladstone's 14 hectares feature similar soil types to Martinborough, but Christine believes the area is possibly a tad warmer, a little wetter, being closer to the Tararua Range, and certainly less windy. Dennis Roberts planted Sauvignon Blanc, Riesling, Pinot Gris and Bordeaux reds. Christine has expanded Gladstone's planting with a block on Dakins Road, a few kilometres away, and included Pinot Noir.

Christine Kernohan: 'I've tried to stay with aromatic whites. There's a logic to what I've got. I've built on what was here already, but I've tried to make it more coherent groups. I've always believed in Riesling, although it's harder to sell. In terms of reds, I'm a great Merlot fan. I make what I like and I'd probably drink a Merlot before I'd drink a Pinot Noir very often. We're doing Pinot too. That's really market pressure.

'With a café, we like to give visitors a choice.'

Gladstone Wines

Chardonnay, Pinot Gris and Sauvignon Blanc are Gladstone's star performers, but there are no duds. If you stop by for lunch, try them all.

Fairmont's Wines

The range includes Chardonnay, Pinot Noir (70 per cent of planting), Sauvignon Blanc and, strongest of the line-up, Riesling.

Fairmont Estate

Jon McNab nurses a cup of tea in the bright kitchen of his renovated country cottage. Through the open door is his red barn winery. He's a particularly focussed young man. But his focus is his wine: not industry politics.

Jon McNab: 'In 1992, I was an exchange student in Sweden. I read in the English magazines that the New Zealand wine industry had a rosy future. I was wanting to get into something either outdoorsy or sporty. So I basically sent off a few letters to various wineries around the country. Martinborough Vineyard replied to say they had a truck driver's job going. I left Wellington for that. At the time I had no idea of the good, the bad or the ugly. So I was really fortunate to do my so-called apprenticeship with Larry McKenna.'

After a couple of years, Jon felt the need to spread his wings. He took a job as assistant winemaker in a South German winery.

Jon McNab: 'It was right on the border with Switzerland on Lake Constance. I wouldn't call it a great growing area, but it was different from New Zealand and I picked up different things on how to make wine. Like with Martinborough [Vineyard], I was jack-of-all-trades. It was a small, two hundred tonne winery, so I got to see everything, but it was pretty tough getting off the plane speaking no German.'

His experience, and Jon reckons, good references, gained him entry to Lincoln University's post-graduate wine science course. In 1996, he was back to help Larry with Martinborough Vineyard's biggest vintage to date. During that time, and before he returned to Germany for another stint, Jon planted Fairmont Estate. His family had owned and holidayed on the property for nearly 20 years.

Jon McNab: 'It was fortunate this terrace just seemed ideal. Gladstone next door was already going. Dennis and Richard had opened the doors to the area. They were the first ones to plant and get recognition for certain wines like Sauvignon Blanc.

I would love to have planted Gewürz, but consistently, year after year it crops lousy. Even though you can make great wine from it, the bottom line is, it has to make some money.

'Rhone-style Syrah has potential here. Not the concentrated Aussie-style though. You have to be open to styles and to change, but I aim at a fruit-driven, multi-dimensional style. But you have to watch you don't overdo the complexity and especially the mushroomy characters. New Pinot Noir drinkers are looking for fruit. They are used to, say, an Aussie Shiraz, which is big, fruity and one-dimensional.

'However, benchmark Pinots are always hard to describe. They are so complex and multi-layered. That's what makes a good Pinot Noir. Many layers, but none standing out.

'I'm happy with thirty acres and I'd rather stay small. The beauty about New Zealand is that we can produce the fruit with ease: and good fruit.'

Bud burst. *Suellen Boag*

Mebus Wine

To date, the brothers have produced a Sauvignon Blanc and a Cab Sav/Merlot/Malbec blend, with a stand-alone Merlot on the way. In the barrel, the Merlot excited them the most.

From left Hidde and Michael Mebus, Mebus Estate. *Pam Ryan*

Mebus Estate

Art history and economics are not the usual background disciplines for viticulturists or winemakers. But then brothers Michael and Hidde Mebus hadn't intended getting into the wine business. That's despite their family owning a farm in Portugal, complete with olive grove, cork oaks and a vineyard. They found the heat there just too much to work in. However, when they took the plunge and starting looking for the perfect vineyard site here, they picked what they maintain is one of the hottest spots in the Wairarapa.

Michael Mebus: 'We picked this spot rather than Martinborough because it has less wind, it's just as dry, the land is cheaper, and it's slightly warmer. The [Ruamahanga] river flows around Dakins Road, and pulls the frost away a bit too. Although we got touched up last year, and that was a nasty shock.'

Michael preceded Hidde from their native Holland by two years. Their father had just died and their mother, a Kiwi, had moved back home.

Michael fell in love with the country, but before he could start the farming course he'd decided on, he met Stan Chifney and worked for him for four years. Stan taught him the basics of wine-making and biochemistry. Michael persuaded Hidde to join him, and the brothers embarked on a search for their own vineyard.

Hidde Mebus: 'Michael got all the soil charts and climate charts. The next step was knocking on a farmer's door and asking if we could dig some holes in his land. Most people bought land because there was a vineyard next door. They didn't always think for themselves. Now seven hundred or eight hundred acres are going in around us, and they are quite big plantings.'

The pair bought 46 hectares, and from 1996 began planting a few hectares each year. Their varietal range is wide: Chardonnay, Merlot and Pinot Noir the largest plantings, with smaller blocks of Sauvignon Blanc, Cabernet Sauvignon, Malbec and Pinot Gris.

Michael Mebus: 'In Europe, people choose wine on region, not variety. They wouldn't know the variety. Our preference is Merlot. We love it and it goes well in this area. But whatever the punter wants to drink is fine with us. Pinot Noir is the "in" variety, but in a hot year it could be overcooked.

'We blend Cab Sav, Merlot and Malbec, but the Malbec we will get rid of. We'll graft Pinot Noir onto it.'

As with their planting, the Mebuses' winery has gone up in stages, too. The grand plan includes an underground cellar, gravity fed winery, cellar door shop and conference room gazing across the picturesque Ruamahanga valley. It's a very pretty setting.

The Mebus boys kicked off the vineyards in their immediate area, and the district could soon rival the Martinborough area for volume. That raises the question of denomination.

Hidde Mebus: 'In years to come, the denomination will be Wairarapa, and if people want to specify, it will be Martinborough, Gladstone, Opaki, or Dakins Road. But the important thing is the quality of the wine.'

Borthwick Estate

Paddy Borthwick doesn't signal his vineyard with neon signs. In fact, screened by a belt of trees down a long driveway, it's pretty hard to find. Paddy's not that flashy either. Laid-back and quietly spoken, he seems most comfortable working the vines. He lets his wine do the talking, and Paddy produces quite a range: a Cab Sav/Merlot/Malbec blend, Chardonnay, Pinot Noir, Riesling, Sauvignon Blanc, and Sangiovese. The latter is rare in New Zealand, but the most widely planted variety in Italy.

Paddy is a local lad. His family has long worked a sheep station. His father felt diversification was prudent, so Paddy took himself off to Roseworthy, then worked all over Australia before doing vintages in France, Switzerland and the United States. On his return, he made his name crafting superb Sauvignon Blanc in Marlborough, working first for Vintech, then Allan Scott. In 1996 he returned home.

Paddy Borthwick: 'We went out and bought this land especially. The farmer who owned the land here split it up into big fifty to one hundred acre blocks. That gives you enough to be viable. We could expand, but before going further it's good to get on top of your first vineyard. Within this vineyard we have a huge variation of soils anyway.

'Single vineyard wines can be great, but I don't know how consistent the quality of a single vineyard is going to be year to year. And that consistency is a very important part, especially in the early stages, of building a name.

'There's room here for both Burgundian and Bordeaux in Wairarapa, especially as our growing season is longer here than Europe. It's very early to tell definitively yet anyway. We'll concentrate on Pinot Noir but Merlot looks very good. Fourteen months in the barrel to go yet. Another two months and then we'll bottle it. Regionality will show in all varieties.'

For Paddy, the district he's chosen has huge advantages and potential, but where it fits in the greater Wairarapa scheme of things is something that will play out over the next few years.

Paddy Borthwick: 'Dakins Road is great but it's still a small piece of the jigsaw. I take a long term view. I think Wairarapa will be the brand, but overseas buyers will just think New Zealand.

'We have an expansive area and all the vineyards have space to be different. We all get on well. We are all new. But that's the hard part about coming to a new area. You look at someone next door who has only been there a year or two and you have to make assumptions about what might do well. But every year you gain a bit more, learn a bit more. That's one reason we spread the varieties.

'It's a good area with good dirt, and a microclimate like Martinborough. The beauty of this area is the expansive potential and the good source of quality water from the river. With free-draining soil, we can monitor moisture and vine stress.

'It's pretty multinational around here. Scottish, German, Dutch, Greek. Maybe we'll call it Five Nations Avenue. Long-term, we'd like to see a wine circuit. But some days it's quite nice not having a lot of people around. Sure, a cellar door builds your brand, but it's nice not to have too much "road noise" in the back of your head and to have the winery to yourself. It can be too full-on.

'It's all about making some quality wine and having some fun. You've got to enjoy it as well at the end of the day. A lot of work but a lot of fun.'

Petrie Vineyard

Spring 2000: one a.m. on a slightly frosty morning. A clamorous roar from somewhere down the Waingawa River provokes a flurry of calls to local police. Two a.m.: Neil Petrie is woken and told of complaints from as far away as Masterton, some four kilometres from his offending turbo blower.

Neil could hear it himself by then: six kilometres further away again! Utilising the expertise and experience of his long-time irrigation contractor Dennis Ordish, some time ago Neil had installed an experimental hot-air vineyard frost protection system. One of the pipes had just blown a joint.

John Petrie: 'After that incident, Dad and Dennis got all these phone calls from people enquiring about the system. So nothing like bad publicity. That was all in the experimental stage. We pretty much have it sorted now. For the last two years we haven't had frost damage here. We did before.'

Neil and Dennis's system blows hot air through the vineyard's irrigation pipes. That raises the temperature around the vines, and more importantly, creates an air flow. Frost can't cope with air flow, let alone a warm one, and the embryonic grapes live to flourish another day.

Sadly, Neil didn't live to see his system brought to full potential, but the vineyard he initiated was already making its presence felt.

John Petrie: 'Dad was first approached in 1990 by Palliser. They wanted shareholders. Dad thought, "What's the point of being a shareholder when we can do it ourselves?"

'I got back from the UK and said, "I don't really want to go hill country farming". We've got another two hundred and fifty acres just over the back of Perry's Road too, but couldn't really make a good living off it. Dad said, "Why don't you have a look at grapes?" It was just after the big pull-out I guess, and there was a real low ebb about the industry. The Martinborough people gave us twenty different answers. So I went up to the Hawkes Bay, I knew a few people there. It was the same there. I got up to Auckland, and I said to Kate Gibbs (eventually our first viticulturist), "What's going on here? Should we be doing this?" She said, "This is probably the best time to do it. But go for the quality end of the market."

'We had a lot of the posts. They're not the prettiest. They're the thinnings from plantations out at Dad's farm. We had our own digger. So we pretty much did it all ourselves. The only thing we felt we should really spend our money on was grafted rootstock. We went all the way there. But we felt we established it pretty economically.

'I was being a wee bit cautious and that's why we started small. But we had all this land to fill. I didn't want to become a fruit salad vineyard: small with a bit of everything. We knew Martinborough was doing well with Pinot Noir and Chardonnay. Kate said Riesling is underrated. So we put some of that in.'

John's vineyard has certainly taken off since then, with more vines planted every couple of years. John doesn't make wine. He simply grows 28 hectares of exceptionally good grapes, supplying Matua Valley, Ata Rangi and Trinity Hills. Some is blended, but his grapes appear in single vineyard wines from all three wineries: Ata Rangi Petrie Chardonnay, Matua Wairarapa Pinot Noir and Innovator Riesling, and Trinity Hills Wairarapa Riesling.

Manager on Duty:

Marion Deimling

No liquor will be sold
and no tastings for:

- people under age
- intoxicated

Schubert Wines

Marion Deimling,
Schubert Wines. *Pam Ryan*

Kai Schubert is a big man. His small cottage at the end of Cambridge Road, seems barely able to contain his stature, and his articulate ebullience. His reputation for crafting superb, concentrated, full-bodied reds is burgeoning by the vintage too.

Kai Schubert: 'Pinot Noir is my favourite variety. It was just a hobby at school, but I did an apprenticeship in wine-making and studied at Geisenheim Viticultural institute. Then I worked in Oregon. Every time I travelled it would be to a wine area, and I was always looking for land suitable for Pinot Noir. Finally I found Wairarapa and that was an

Schubert Wines

Difficult to find a weak one. Look for the 2000 Cabernet Sauvignon; 2003 Royal Easter Show Trophy winner in the Cabernet or Cabernet predominant blend section: exceptional.

eye-opener. Such a young area but producing Pinot Noir with such intensity in colour, structure and tannins. We bought the small plot in Martinborough and the large one in Taratahi.'

The one-and-a-quarter hectare Martinborough plot was already in vines: Pinot Noir, Müller Thurgau, Syrah, a few rows of the ubiquitous Mystery Red, Merlot and Chardonnay. Twelve hectares of mainly Pinot Noir, planted on the Dakins Road plot in 1999, was hit by frost, destroying its first crop.

Kai Schubert: 'We were in a Sydney restaurant crying about the fact that we had to wait so long for a first fruit, and by coincidence at the next table was a winemaker from the Gimblett Gravels district in Hawkes Bay. He offered to sell us some fruit. It was not the normal type of supply contract. We got an allocation of so many rows. We could decide on picking days and leaf plucking.'

The Cabernet Sauvignon, Cabernet Franc and Syrah made from those Hawkes Bay grapes immediately and resoundingly established the newcomer's label. The first Schubert Pinot Noir, grown at Dakins Road, confirmed it was no fluke. But Kai doesn't let his Pinot passion dilute his enthusiasm for his other wines: Chardonnay, a Cab Sav/Merlot, and Tribianco: a crisp Chardonnay/Pinot Gris/Müller Thurgau blend.

Kai Schubert: 'There's a lot of fermentation CO_2 still in there [Tribianco] because we avoid pumping. The wine is given quite some time for maturation – which helps combine the CO_2 into the liquid. For instance, we release the 2000 whites when other people release the 2001. For aging, it is quite nice, because it has a refreshing spritz, especially in summer, and it's different in style. A hint of barrique, nutty, pear, and fresh white fruit. There's honey character too. Good with sushi. You need some air to bring the fruit out. That's a sign that wine is aging well.

'Our Chardonnay is different in style. I don't like the overwhelming buttery type. You want some fruit – lemon, lime, melon – but of course in combination with some roasty aromas from the oak. It was half fermented in stainless steel, and half in new and used French oak. Also there is some mixing of lees. We didn't inoculate for maleolactic [fermentation] but the barrels might have done a little. The end is a honeyed character but nutty and creamy.

'We make our Cabernet Sauvignon in a Pinot Noir method. Normally you would crush the berries and have no cold maceration, with pump-overs to get more air into the system.

'With us the berries are still intact when put into open fermentation vats for cold maceration, to promote fruitiness and carbonic maceration within the berries. We want tannins out of skins rather than pips, and no pumping. Crushing only really happens with pigeage [punching down the cap of wine skins] within fermentation. After fermentation we leave the wine on the skins for a week or two before pressing.

'We wanted to avoid the green pepper, paprika characters of unripe Cabernet Sauvignon. We aim for tobacco, chocolate, blackcurrant and boysenberry. There's very little Merlot in this. Fourteen and a half per cent alcohol is a bit too high. Maybe we left the fruit to get too ripe. We choose Burgundian barrels, because the oak integrates much better in the wine than the barriques from Bordeaux coopers.'

Past misfortunes prompted Kai to invest in some prophylactic technology. A wind machine protected the Dakins Road block from spring 2002 on. Just as well. Severe frosts that same season meant no grapes from Hawkes Bay for the 2003 vintage.

Kai's partner, Marion Deimling, is also a winemaker. If two winemakers are better than one, three is pure luxury, and the pair are sometimes assisted by Hiro Kusuda. Only the fourth or fifth Japanese to study at Geisenheim, Hiro initially joined Kai to conduct research for his thesis for the institute. Smitten by the Pinot bug, he leased Muirlea Vineyard for a time and launched his Kusuda label. Now using Schubert fruit, Hiro makes his wine at Kai's winery in Greytown, and looks after Schubert's marketing in Japan.

That's two up-and-coming labels definitely worth keeping an eye on.

'That's why it's called Solstone: Sol for the sun
— and the stones. And of course we are in the
Solway area.' Elizabeth Barrett-Hackel

Masterton

Solstone Estate Winery

While the industry at large woos the export market, Solstone looks to Masterton. And it's more than a cellar door, with its gift shop, café, function venue, a unique customised labelling service for corporates, weddings and gifts and even an historical corner. Masquerade balls and 'Wine Down Days' offering live music, and a hot air balloon fiesta are all part of Solstone's active annual programme.

Solstone began life in 1981 as Bloomfields Vineyard, the reincarnation of Lamb's original nineteenth century Solway vineyard nearby. Lloyd Hackel and his wife Elizabeth Barrett-Hackel took over in 2001. It soon became apparent to them that half the community had some sort of stake in the place.

Elizabeth Barrett-Hackel: 'It's rare that you meet an old resident of Masterton who didn't have a hand in helping set up this vineyard. It obviously became quite a community project. We had a philosophy of "Don't change anything for the sake of changing, and don't change anything in the first year", but we thought we would eventually restructure the vineyard, and maybe lease more vines.

'Now we are here, we believe what's more important is the delight in seeing people enjoy the wine (and themselves). It's the involvement with people and the community that gives us a buzz now. This is our retirement hobby. Some people get a lot of pleasure designing a special gift bottle label. We want to enjoy life and offer the same to others. I worked out that if we sold every bottle we currently export, at the cellar door instead, it would be the same as expanding three times: so it makes economic sense too.

Suellen Boag

Solstone Wines

Both the Pinot and Bordeaux styles are consistent performers, and the Chardonnay and Sauvignon Blanc are well rounded and flavourful.

'We also have two contract vineyards: Lyndor and Paulownia Estates. It's a close relationship with them both. We're not just buying the fruit. They're part of the Solstone family.'

There's a warmth about Elizabeth and Lloyd's approach to business that suits the vineyard's name. But in fact it has other origins.

Elizabeth Barrett-Hackel: 'Solstone is a traditional Bordeaux vineyard in varieties and planting style. The fruiting wire is lower than your knee. We are very low cropping in terms of kilos per vine, and pick stones as much as fruit. They keep rising to surface, so we put them under the fruiting wire. There's a real influence from the sun heating the stones and assisting the ripening process. That's why it's called Solstone: Sol for the sun – and the stones. And of course we are in the Solway area.'

Almost half the vineyard is planted in Cabernet Sauvignon: the rest in Merlot, Cabernet Franc, Sauvignon Blanc, Chardonnay and Pinot Noir. Depending on the season, either the Burgundy or Bordeaux styles excel. The French influence was reinforced by winemaker Luc Desbonnets, and the tradition is followed by Bernard Newman, Solstone's new winemaker.

Loopline Vineyard

Frank Parker was always busy: bustling breathlessly between errands: rushing from one business chore to the next. He's still busy enough. He has a vineyard and a winery to run, pretty much single-handed. But it's a laid-back, enjoyable sort of bustle now. Frank's having the time of his life.

Frank Parker: 'It started off as a semi-retirement play around: something to do. I love drinking wine so why don't I have a go at making it? It just grew from there. It's now a business. I didn't do the wine clubs. I was a plonk drinker but wine has so much more character than rum. Every single bottle is individual.

'I needed a change and a challenge before I was too old to enjoy it. I knew the area. It's very dry in summer with very free-draining soil. So

I did a bit of quick research. No consultants or anything like that. Licked my finger and stuck it up in the air. I checked on rainfall. I didn't know that we needed to worry about a frost problem, and we haven't really got a serious one anyway. That was good enough. So I planted.

'At that time, the talk was that there is only one place in the Wairarapa to grow grapes and that's Martinborough. I've always been one for a bit of a challenge, and there is nothing gets me going better than someone saying I can't do it.

'People would say grapes wouldn't grow here because they never had, but Lansdowne is only four kilometres in a straight line from here. There are now nine vineyards in the Opaki area. The largest is a hundred and seventy acres. Those investments are on the strength of what we did here.'

After a false start with a couple of unsuitable varieties, Frank settled on Riesling and Pinot Noir, with smaller plantings of Pinot Gris, Sauvignon Blanc, Chardonnay and Merlot. He picked brains and bought books to build wine-making expertise, but on the mechanical side, he had a head start: Frank had spent most of his life in the automotive engineering trade.

His winery, almost entirely his own creation, cost a fraction of anything of comparable capacity in the area. The labelling machine looks like the prize-winner from a high school wood-working class. He built his own sprayer. The chiller sitting outside the door is an old refrigerated container. The container door was too small for the second-hand stainless tanks to fit through – so Frank cut a hole in the side, shoved the tanks in, then bolted the side back on. Voilà: chillable tanks for a fifth of the new price. His greatest coup, though, is his wine filter: found discarded and apparently 'knackered' outside Stan Chifney's winery. Frank paid Stan $250 and took it away. On his way home, he stopped at a dairy equipment supply merchant, and bought some rubber tubing. Fifteen minutes of lathe work produced the requisite replacement washers, and two hours after his purchase, the filter was in operation.

That mechanical ingenuity is all a means to an end though, and the end is Frank's passion for his wine. Half of his satisfaction comes from chatting at his cellar door.

Frank Parker: 'In the motor trade I was working five days a week, seven hours a day, and it was a bore getting out of bed. Now I'm doing nine or ten hours a day, seven days a week, and loving every minute of it.

'This is a positive business. People love coming to a winery. They have a good time and love taking away the product to repeat the experience.

'People from Masterton going away for a weekend will often come in and buy a bottle or two to take with them. Particularly those going to the Hawkes Bay. They just love going to Hawkes Bay with a Wairarapa wine.'

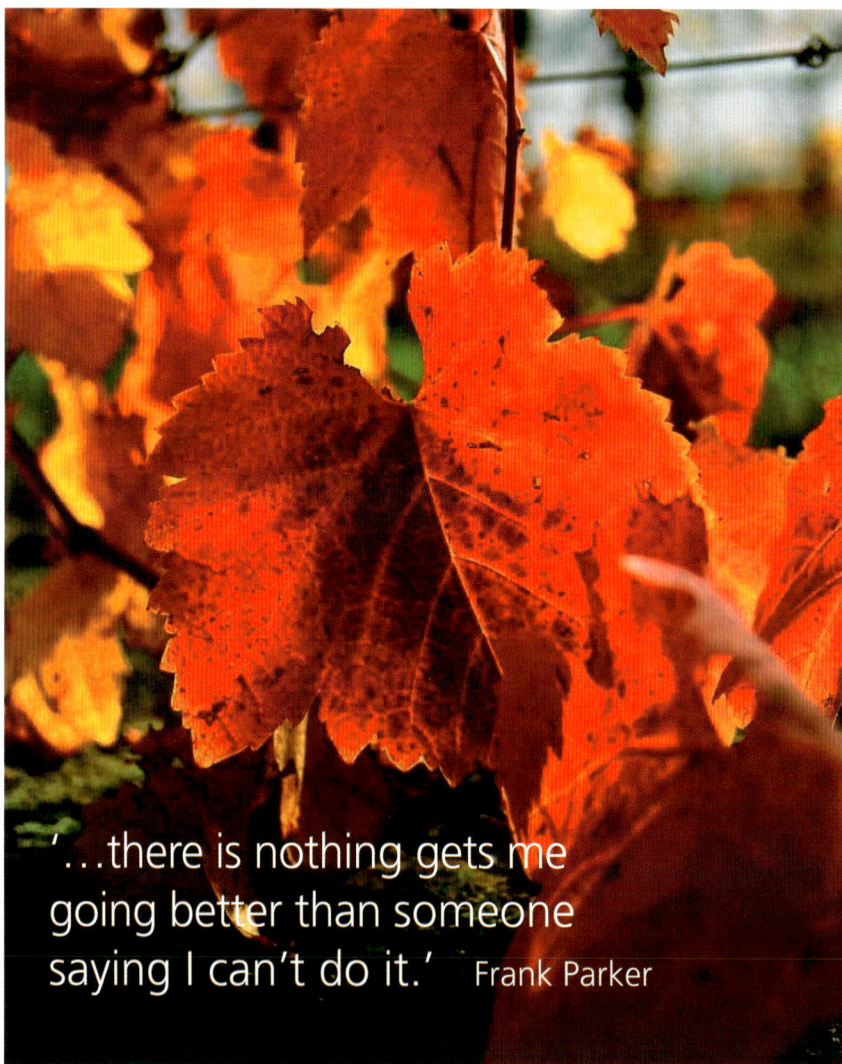

'...there is nothing gets me going better than someone saying I can't do it.' Frank Parker

Pam Ryan

The Outliers

As the Wairarapa wine industry expands and explores new territory, the grape-growing frontier keeps moving. It's too early to say with assurance where it will finish up. Far easier to declare where grapes certainly can't be grown: where rainfall is excessive, or heat accumulation insufficient. But even where the territory for miles around appears utterly unsuitable, pockets of viability may emerge. In any case, there is no accounting for the resourcefulness – not to mention obduracy – of the vinophile spirit.

Bowlands

The tiny, white, pit-sawn board and batten Church of St Francis sits a few hundred metres above Bowlands House, half an hour's drive north-east of Masterton. The breathlessly tranquil churchyard is set about with graves ringed in white stones. Neil Petrie, whose innovative turbo blowers successfully protect his son John's vines along the Waingawa River, rests here under a simple oak cross.

The hills around are a medley of plantation pines and macrocarpa, redwoods, oaks, alders, kahikatea, kanuka, and totara. In the gully below, gaunt poplars compete with hawthorns, manuka and cabbage trees. The terrace behind the church, no more than a couple of football fields in size, is John Falloon's Church of St Francis vineyard. John's business partner Mike Thompson, from Atlanta, actually kicked it off.

John Falloon: 'I always said I'd plant vines by the church. One year we had American guests between Christmas and New Year, and I showed them around the tentative site, telling them that when I had a spare fifty thousand dollars I'd do it. Mike drew me aside and said he'd like to advance the money. I said, "You can't. It's not proven or even investigated". We needed to discuss it further but never did. Then as he was leaving he handed me an envelope enclosing a cheque for fifty thousand dollars … US! He has been back every year touring New Zealand, and even leaf-plucked last year. After a feasibility study with Alan Clarke, we decided we needed another partner, and Frank Olsson, formerly from Sweden and the BNZ in Singapore and Japan but now back in New Zealand, became our third partner.

'We are still working on getting a positive cash flow, and this year's capital expenditure on a frost irrigation system will reduce the risk from frosts that have affected our yields: especially 2003.'

The late autumn sun is struggling to pierce the clear cold air, just a gnat's whisker short of a frost. John is supervising net removal. Harvest is not quite finished, with a late clone Pinot Gris yet to pick. So the gas guns are still primed, and their booms echo around the hills like ball-bearings on a corrugated iron roof.

John has two clones of Pinot Gris by the churchyard and several hectares of Pinot Noir up past the old Bowlands shearing shed. He sells his fruit to Te Kairanga, but takes back some wine, which is sold to clients of his wife Philippa's corporate retreat business.

John Falloon: 'It's hard enough learning to grow grapes, without also learning to make wine. I've never been involved in a crop before where one mistake or event can cause the lot to be spoiled. It's been a massive learning curve. Great fun.'

So Bowlands isn't on the label yet, but maybe sometime when John has the time, and a spare few dollars…

Wycroft

Lawrie Bryant keeps a splendid cellar. It's frequently in demand. Lawrie and his wife Sally are assiduous hosts. Their house guest this week is Henry Blofeld: cricketing commentator, wine writer and bon vivant. Unfortunately, Henry's paramount wish right now remains unfulfilled. Lawrie's Wycroft Pinot Noir, the first vintage from the initial 1200 vines planted just through the garden hedge from the house, was only bottled today. Henry flies back to Britain tomorrow morning.

Lawrie Bryant: 'The fellow at the bottling plant told me that Pinot, and I suspect some other wines, goes into "bottle shock" for a time after bottling. He said a week or two after bottling you might well wonder why you bothered, and you just have to wait for it to climb out of that state. That's why makers hold them back from release until they've settled. I would hate you to judge our wine on an unsettled youngster.'

No number of indignant 'my dear old thing's will sway Lawrie. Wycroft the First will remain untouched until the blessed hand of time has bestowed at least a vestige of maturity.

Wycroft is at Matahiwi, west of Masterton, further west, Lawrie points out, than any other planting. The Tararuas loom large. More rain would be expected here than even a few kilometres to the east. Nonetheless, heat accumulation is good, and the fruit ripens well. But as with all of the Wairarapa, frost ever lurks in spring.

Lawrie Bryant: 'We picked one day earlier than last year, at higher brix and enhanced flavours, but only a third of the crop. Appalling frost damage. A very strange year indeed. From the winemaker's appraisal, it had looked as though our crop would be about half as much again as last year but it was not to be. Such is the lot of agricultural risk.'

Homeburn Station

Tucked up against the Haurangi Forest Park, almost as far as White Rock on the south Wairarapa coast, is Homeburn Station: a rugged mix of creek flats, rough paddocks, bush-covered hills and the most southern vineyard in the North Island. Paul and Cherry Cutfield run cattle, sheep, and a pig or two, cut a bit of firewood, and feast on venison and wild pork whenever they want. Pinot Noir just seemed to fit.

Paul Cutfield: 'When we went to Spain, we were inspired. Over there, there are little groves everywhere. It's not the monoculture you have here. We wanted to make wine for ourselves in that European family tradition: family and friends gathering to pick and make wine. We thought, "We're not looking for the Wairau Valley here. We just want a little terrace," and we knew this place was here. A little nichey block. We checked the soil and found it was suitable.

'I planted the vines like specimen trees in the botanic gardens. With every one, the roots had to be laid out and unmatted. At the bottom was a handful of lime and fertiliser. Then the bucket load of compost. And they just rocketed.

'Having these vines is like having a thousand mistresses and they're all on the phone on the same night. There's room to triple the number of vines. But that's a lot of mistresses! Anyway, we use a low trellising system. You wouldn't want any more than a thousand vines or you'd do your back in.

'Being given the first bottle of our own Pinot was like being handed a baby!'

Paul and Cherry make the wine themselves. But Clive Paton was one of Paul's university mates, and Grant Stanley, assistant winemaker at Ata Rangi, is a close friend. They've both been generous with help and advice.

The new chiller/killing shed complex by the barn is a good, clean place to do things. Fermentation heat is supplied by a wrap-around electric blanket. A garden sprinkler cools things down when required. The kegs are placed in a large insulated box with a small heater to see the wine through maleolactic fermentation.

There's no intention to sell the wine, so a label is still very much a loose idea: very loose.

Pam Ryan

Paul Cutfield: 'It could be Pink Pig Pinot. My yearly prank is dyeing the pigs pink. They come out neon for a week or two.

Pink or not, the Cutfields' Pinot fits right into their epicurean lifestyle.

Paul Cutfield: 'Often we sit up overlooking the vineyard with friends, a bottle of wine and our hors d'oeurvy things, and watch the sun go down. Then on dusk the whole place erupts into native birdsong.'

Cherry Cutfield: 'This is not Tuscany. This is a quintessentially wild native spot: a vineyard in a bush setting. Kowhai flowering in the spring, and the wonderful red rewarewa, then cabbage trees and snow white manuka following. We did think we might sneak a few hundred Russell lupins onto the bank though, just to remind us of the South Island.'

Toast

We set out from Memorial Square replete with festival wine glasses and ribboned holders, looking for a bank to stock up on 'Festival Francs'. The day, dry so far, carries the cool whiff of moisture on the wind, but the walk down Kitchener Street is convivial and warming. Visitors mill about getting their bearings, and organising rendezvous in case they are separated.

Then we are into the thick of it. A kaleidoscope of tastes and tipples: music and merriment. Toast Martinborough is like a rich fruitcake: a heady but carefully crafted mix of food, wine, jolly company and boisterous entertainment.

Burnt Spur, our first chance to taste, is chock-a-block. A short stroll further is Palliser Estate and their yeasty Méthode Champenoise is a sparkling starter. The West Coast whitebait fritters provide a perfect match. The Beat Girls are jumping on the mobile stage as we down the last of a delectable Pinot Gris and catch a shuttle bus.

At Nga Waka, the Chardonnay and grilled flounder sandwich seem meant for each other. Outside, Shaun Preston lets rip with another Elton John number, as we collide (literally) with old Auckland mates on the grass dance 'floor'. We sample Nga Waka's first Pinot Noir at Toast and compare notes.

The samba rhythms pulsing from Voss Estate's site attract us to a cluster of festival marquees around the corner. Over the road at Muirlea, Shawn Brown reckons Willie would have rated this the best Toast so far, and there are four of the late winemaker's Pinot vintages on offer! The filo chicken and peach is shared around, as the day settles in to a smorgasbord of sampling, sharing and sipping: scintillating food and wine matches interrupted only by gentle walks or short bus rides between vineyards.

The Beat Girls at Palliser Estate, Toast Martinborough. *Alan Knowles*

Margrain, Martinborough Vineyard, Claddagh, Alana, Te Kairanga and Murdoch James: each offers its own Bacchic alchemy of food, wine and music.

Our perambulatory banquet is cruising into late afternoon as we settle in front of the Ata Rangi stage. The irrepressible Janice Gray is winding us up, and the exquisite Célèbre is settling us down, as we sample Ruth Pretty's traditional fruit cake.

———

Busloads troop back over the hill, glowing and sated. They'll return: some to another Toast, others to investigate the wider Wairarapa, reconnoitring new vineyards and knocking on more recently hung cellar doors. Their curiosity and enthusiasm will pervade wine shops, tasting rooms, and cellars; fill restaurant tables and wine websites; infiltrate lunches, barbeques, and picnics, in ever more parts of the globe. The wine may hail from

Puruatanga Road or over Gladstone way; from Te Muna Terrace or East Taratahi. The label might say Wairarapa, Martinborough, Masterton or indeed name places yet unplanted.

But wherever glasses are swirled, and palates quicken, and the elixir of the grape is savoured, the wines will summon memories of the faces, vineyards and voices; from those hot plains, over the hills from Wellington.

Above:
'Come sample my wares,' Toast.
Alan Knowles

Right:
A visitor from the Hawkes Bay, Toast. *Alan Knowles*

Glossary

Barrique: Originally confined to Bordeaux's 225-litre oak casks, but now applied to new oak barrels in which wine is matured or fermented.

Brix: A scale for determining the approximate concentration of sugars in grapes. One degree brix corresponds approximately to 18 grams of sugar per litre.

Cellar door: Where wine is sold directly from a winery.

ISO 9002 & ISO 14001: Internationally recognised standards of quality in a wine.

Field grafting: Where fruit-bearing scion material is grafted onto phyloxera resistant rootstock in the field, as opposed to indoors (bench grafting). Known also as field budding.

Maceration: Where the grape solids (skins, seeds and stems) are steeped in the juice to extract flavours, tannins and colour.

Must: The intermediate mixture of liquid and solids between juice and wine: crushed, chopped or mashed fruit being prepared for, or undergoing fermentation.

Pigeage: Punching down the cap of wine skins on top of a fermenting tank, to encourage aeration and extraction of tannins and colour.

Transfer pot: A receptacle for moving must or wine between tanks. Use of it avoids pumping.

Veraison: The beginning of ripening when grapes change from a hard green state to become softer and coloured.

Clone: A genetically identical plant obtained by taking cuttings from an original 'mother vine'. There may be many clones of a single variety; e.g. Dijon clones of Chardonnay and Pinot Noir from Burgundy. Abel and 10-5 are two Pinot Noir clones grown widely in Martinborough.

Clonal selection: Choosing which clones to plant or include in a wine.

Martinborough

for Peter Black and Mary Macpherson

A town planned on the Union Jack,
streets named after Mr Martin's
grand tour, eighteen seventy-nine–
Panama, Texas, New York – gives way to

harp after harp of wires and vines. At
Walkers', a dachshund keeps the birds off,
nibbles the lowest grapes as they ripen.
A cutting they thought Syrah grew into

something entirely Unknown: They name
the wine Justa Red or Notre Vigne,
startlers that leap the fence and gallop
into the drinkable blue-black night–

the rest of the flag. Not many cars.
A few farms, like stars, to steer by.

by Andrew Johnston
(from *Birds of Europe Poems*,
Victoria University Press, 2000.)

.